A BIOGRAPHICAL STORY

INTO AFRICA

EGON FALK

Copyright © Egon Falk 2021
Published by BUOY MEDIA LLC
https://www.buoy-media.com

No part of this book may be reproduced, scanned, or distributed in any printed or electronic form without permission from the author.

The Author holds exclusive rights to this work. Unauthorized duplication is prohibited.
All rights reserved.

Cover design by Juan Villar Padron
https://www.juanjpadron.com

Photo credit to Lee Bailey
http://leebaileyphotography.com/

Special thanks to my editor Janell Parque
http://janellparque.blogspot.com/

CONTENTS

Acknowledgments	5
1. MBEYA TANZANIA	13
2. TO NORWAY AND NEW CHALLENGES	26
3. PIONEERING IN AFRICA	28
Culture Shock and Primitive Living.	
4. CRUSADES	35
The birth of new life outreach	
5. SIGNS, WONDERS, AND HEALINGS	37
6. THE THINGS WHICH ARE SEEN WERE NOT MADE OF THINGS WHICH ARE VISIBLE	46
By Pastor Frede Rasmussen	
7. CONFRONTATIONS AND RIOTS	53
8. WHAT IS A MIRACLE?	63
9. THE DANISH AFRICAN	82
By Pastor Geir Stomnås	
10. THE MASAI TRIBE	86
11. EXTRAORDINARY AND POWERFUL MIRACLES	95
12. THE IMPOSSIBLE BECOMES POSSIBLE	111
Healed of HIV/AIDS - and resurected from the dead...	
13. DR. EGON FALK - THE FISHERMAN OF PEOPLE	117
By Pastor Gunnar Jeppestøl	
14. THE CHILDREN OF MY HEART	121
Verner from Kibondo and the others...	
15. THE SMELL OF AFRICA	126
By Nick Hansen, Chairman of the Board of New Life Outreach DK.	
16. FOR GOD EVERYTHING IS POSSIBLE	137
Bring Dr. Egon back to Iaela.	
17. THE ZANZIBAR CRUSADES	143
18. THE ACADEMY OF LEADERSHIP	151
By Professor Oyvind Garder Anderson	
19. SMALL BEGINNINGS	160

20. A CHILD OF A MISSIONARY   169
   By Tina Falk, Hannah & Egon's firstborn child
21. A MISSIONARY CHILD'S SCHOOL TALE   178
   By Ruben Falk, son of Hannah & Egon Falk
22. BUSH BABY   188
   By Gitte Falk Jakobsen, Hannah & Egon's youngest child
23. MARRIED TO EGON   191
   By Hannah Esbensen Falk

Help make a difference   197
About the Author   201

ACKNOWLEDGMENTS

BY REINHARD BONNKE:

Since you now hold the book about Dr. Egon Falk's life and ministry in your hands, I can tell you the following: Dr. Egon Falk from Arusha in Tanzania goes back and forth in East Africa with his New Life Outreach Crusades. His teams and he conduct up to eighteen campaigns a year, often under extremely difficult conditions. Yet, they are extremely fruitful.

The world famous evangelist Reinhard Bonnke and his wife Anny Bonnke was good friends with Hannah and Egon Falk. Reinhard Bonnke died December 7, 2019 in Florida.

Many people receive Jesus Christ as their Lord and Savior and are added to the local body of believers.

God's hand is upon his life and ministry. I can recommend to the whole body of Christ that they, through intercession and finances, support this humble servant of God.

ACKNOWLEDGMENTS

BY ARIL EDVARDSEN.

I am very happy that we now have a book about Dr. Egon Falk´s ministry.

Lots of Scandinavian preachers read only the Scriptures about Philip and the revival in Samaria. They preach only that signs, wonders, and miracles took place as Philip preached the Good News of the Anointed One.

But Dr. Egon Falk is a missionary/evangelist who continuously EXPERIENCES what Philip experienced in chapter 8 of the Acts of the Apostles.

Dr. Egon Falk is called the second Reinhard Bonnke of Africa. This is a misleading description, however. Though, without a doubt, it is well-intended. Dr. Egon Falk is not a carbon copy; he is an original man of God.

Aril Edvardsen was a norwegian pastor and author. He founded Troens Bevis World Evangelisation in 1965. He died, 69 years old, September 6. 2008 while traveling in Kenya.

Most Scandinavians are probably not aware that we have this international missionary/evangelist with such a ministry for the Lord Jesus.

He conducts large crusades all over East Africa. Thousands seek salvation during his meetings, and Jesus reveals himself through healings, signs, and wonders.

I have known Dr. Egon and his wife Hannah for many years and watched their service growing richer and stronger to the honor of God. Together, we have held several crusades and preachers' seminars in Tanzania.

It is going to be an inspiration to many, especially to the "new generation," and it will demonstrate how God wants to use young Christians in the global harvest at the end of this age.

ACKNOWLEDGMENTS

BY ARNE BAKKEN:

Ever since becoming a Christian, I have longed to see Acts of the Apostles in our days. When I started reading the Biblical accounts of how Jesus performed wonders and how the first body of believers managed to live, it created a desire, a longing in me to experience the living Jesus today. I have seen healings, and I have seen people seek God in many meetings since I was born again in 1976. But it was not until 1991 when Aril Edvardsen invited me to join him on a crusade to the Muslim town Tanga in Tanzania, that this desire was really fulfilled.

Arne Bakken had a past as a drug addict, but was saved in the 1970s. For several years he traveled around in Norway and visited schools with the Marita film about drugs destructive effect. He died in 2001.

In this crusade, where sometimes 60-70,000 people were gathered (the total population was 150,000), I finally experienced what I had been longing for during the 15 preceding years. The only way I can describe what happened is like boarding a time-traveling device and waking up in Jerusalem as described in Acts of the Apostles chapters 2 through 5.

The lame walked, the blind saw, cripples were healed, and the demon-possessed were delivered. Tens of thousands of people sought salvation over a span of a few days.

In this crusade, I met Dr. Egon and his wife, Hannah Falk. They had arranged the crusade, and we got well acquainted during the week it occurred. I realized from what they said that this was more or less an everyday occurrence in their ministry as evangelists in Tanzania. A year later, I returned to Tanzania for a Crusade, which New Life Outreach had arranged. In this crusade, miracles happened similar to the last time. Signs, wonders, and healings took place in every meeting, and thousands were saved.

ACKNOWLEDGMENTS

Dr. Egon and Hannah Falk are from Denmark. God has called them for incredible work in East Africa. After hearing their story and experiencing their meetings, I got a strong desire to let other Christians in on their life and service.

Dr. Egon and Hannah Falk are good friends of mine. I want you to get to know them, too. I also want to encourage you to become intercessors and support partners for them in their further thrust toward gatherings.

BY DR. EGON FALK:

These three men of God wrote this (the previous three testimonials) to me before they went to be with the Lord Jesus, and I honor their lives and ministries.

BY PASTOR SAM CARR:

"As a minister of the Gospel for over 40 years, I have watched ministries come and go, rise and fall.

I have had the privilege of observing and participating with Evangelist Dr. Egon Falk for many of those years, and

I have watched a man of destiny press through and accomplish what many just dream of doing in a lifetime.

Sam Carr is the founder of Word of Life Center in Shreveport, Louisiana, USA.

His sacrifice to go to Tanzania and lay down roots to build a work for God is truly incredible. Only eternity will tell of the magnitude of the impact he has made in that nation and many other nations around the world.

He has a story to tell of the Glory of God and His faithfulness.

Take hold of his story and let it inspire you to reach higher for the Kingdom and Glory of God."

ACKNOWLEDGMENTS

BY PASTOR DAVID HANSEN:

Dr. Egon, you are braver than me; you go out where nobody else went, where nobody else thought it possible.

You've broken through in closed areas, lifted up people who were weighed down, stood the test where others broke down, loved where hatred ruled, forgiven where bitterness had its root, stepped up against Satan's threats and powers, and broken the chains of poverty.

It's an honor to be your friend!

David Hansen is a pastor and founder of Aalborg Menigheds Center.

BY PASTOR JAN HALVORSEN:

I came to visit Dr. Egon and Hannah Falk in Tanzania for the first time in 1991. It was powerful to meet with Africa and the African culture, but even more powerful to experience the world of miracles! I had experienced miracles earlier, but what we saw in our first crusade in Korogwe was overwhelming.

After Dr. Egon finished preaching about Jesus, who lives today and wants to

Jan Halvorsen is the Pastor at the Zoé Church in Fredrikstad, Norway.

save and heal people, we experienced how powerful miracles began to happen. The first night, a little deaf and dumb girl was healed. For the next few evenings, she came to the platform and danced with joy with us at the end of the meetings. There was great joy and excitement for Jesus! Her father stood on the ground and beamed with joy!

One mama carried her child, sick with cancer, to the first crusade meeting. The girl had a big tumor on her side, which weighed several kilos. After the meeting, the mom carried her

ACKNOWLEDGMENTS

back home, and the girl looked very sick. But after a while, she asked to be let down; she did not want her mom to carry her. She wanted to walk. The mom let her down, and she was totally healed. The next day, they came to the crusade and testified, filled with excitement about the healing, and the tumor was gone.

Mark 16 says that the believers are to lay hands on the sick, and they shall be healed. This is a promise for all believers, and it gives us boldness to pray for the sick. The Bible also tells us about the gifts of the Spirit that will be given to us in ministry. In Acts 8, we read about the evangelist Philip who was in Samaria. Many people with unclean spirits were set free, and many lame and limping people were healed. I have attended many crusades together with Dr. Egon and Hannah, and every time, it hits me—this is the evangelist, Philip! In all the crusades I have attended, I have seen many demon-possessed people set free and many lame and limping throw their sticks and crutches away! They walked, danced, and jumped all over the platform after Jesus healed them.

Some of these crutches and sticks are placed in big jars or hanging on the wall in NLO's office building as a testimony that Jesus is alive today, and He is the same forever! It's obvious that Dr. Egon has an anointing that is similar to what the evangelist Philip had.

At the crusades, I have seen people healed from many different diseases. Small children who never stood on their legs have experienced Jesus' power and began to take their first steps; deaf people have received their hearing, and crippled arms and legs have stretched out and been healed. Since I have kids and grandkids, to see a sick child healed is what touches me the most.

When John the Baptist was in prison, he began to doubt if Jesus really was the Messiah, and he sent his disciples to ask him. "Are you the one to expect, or should we expect someone else"?

Jesus did not say, yes, I am the Messiah, but he said, "Go and tell John the things which you hear and see: the blind see and the lame walk, the lepers are cleansed, and the deaf hear, the dead are raised up, and the poor have the Gospel preached to them." Matt. 11:4-5.

Then John knew that this was the fulfillment of the prophecies about the Messiah from the book of Esaias (Isaiah). It's the same today! When the Gospel is proclaimed with authority and power, God will do wondrous things! He will confirm His own Word.

I have seen blind receive their eyesight, and I remember a big crusade in Mbeya. I believe we had more than 20,000 people attending. At the end of the meeting, a line of people wanted to give their testimony about their healing. The crew organized the line and tried to get a man to attend this line. This man was standing by himself and just looking at the lights and speaker towers. It was as if he did not understand that he had to join the line. Finally, Dr. Egon got to interview this man, and it turned out he was born blind and had never been able to see; now, he stood there and watched lights and colors for the first time. He tried to explain what he saw, but he was almost in shock!

It's difficult to doubt when you see the power of God work this way!

During these almost thirty years I have visited Dr. Egon and Hannah, I have seen many miracles. Mostly sick who have been healed, but also miracles to the weather situation. I remember one crusade at Lake Tanganyika; there were many demon-possessed people and a lot of occult activity. The witch doctors came to stop the crusade. In an odd way, the sky became dark just above the crusade site. The clouds were very heavy, and the water poured down. The crusade crew worked hard to cover the equipment, and we expected the meeting to be over! But, no! Dr. Egon prayed and went against the weather, and the local people began to march at the crusade site. Despite the heavy rain, they sang songs of victory and demanded the rain to stop. The rain stopped, and we had a wonderful meeting.

ACKNOWLEDGMENTS

Signs, wonders, and miracles affirm the Word of God. It creates an open door to the heart, and people receive the Gospel and get saved! Jesus had deep pity for those suffering, and He healed the sick and set the bound free. He is the same today, and He loves to do miracles!

Dr. Egon Falk is a tool in the hand of God. Through his preaching and proclamation of the victory of Jesus Christ and his work of atonement on the cross, God's miracle power is released. Glory to the name of Jesus. The power and praise and glory belong to Him forever!

Chapter One
MBEYA TANZANIA

"BWANA YESU ASIFIWE!" I, Dr. Egon Falk, shout out to more than 70,000 people: "PRAISE THE LORD!" in Kiswahili.

We are in Mbeya, Tanzania. For several days, the New Life Outreach team has been rigging up the equipment from the trucks.

The floodlights hit the crowds that have gathered—another crusade has started. I, Dr. Egon, enter the platform, and people are dancing and waving their scarves and branches broken off from trees. I am ready to preach the Gospel once more. People are excited, and the sick are lined up at the platform. I glance at the crowds, grab my Bible, and start preaching the Good News of Jesus.

But this is not where it all started. I had a long way to go before experiencing a breakthrough in my ministry as a missionary and an evangelist.

CHILDHOOD ON THE ROCKY ISLAND OF BORNHOLM.

I grew up in Denmark in a little fisherman's village called Tejn on the rocky island of Bornholm in the Baltic Sea. My father was a salmon fisherman, and I dreamed of becoming a fisherman like him.

Mom and Dad were Christians, and we prayed a lot, especially for Daddy when he was at sea for long periods of the fishing season.

My grandfather was a Seventh Day Adventist, and my grandmother was a Lutheran. Grandpa suffered from heart disease, so my Dad had to work hard from when he was a small boy to earn money for the whole family, which was rather poor. One day, a preacher from Sweden came to visit the village next to ours. He put up a tent and held revival meetings. Rumor had it that they would be praying for the sick at these meetings. One day, my grandpa asked my grandmother to fetch the preacher and ask him to come and pray for him. "I want him to do nothing but pray for me to get healed. I don't want to hear anything else," he said.

The preacher came to visit my grandpa, and he did not touch any theological subjects—just prayed that my grandpa might get healed. He was healed and baptized in the Holy Spirit with the sign of praying in tongues. Now, my grandpa opened up his house for revival meetings. My grandparents had a big smokehouse where they professionally smoked the fish herring. They all smelled from the herring and smoke, but they experienced the mighty power of God. Some fishermen would go there only to taunt God. But many of those even would fall prostrate, smitten to the ground by the power of God, and get saved.

I grew up as a third-generation in this environment. I had heard my grandparents and my parents tell of these things since my early childhood.

I did not, however, personally relate to all this. I did live in a Christian home and environment, but that is all there is to say about that. I went to Sunday School and listened to lots of Bible stories. But my main reason for going there was to gain stars for my Sunday School Book to win a prize at the seasonal Christmas party.

When my father caught plenty of fish and earned accordingly, I often brought money to give to the Sunday School. That made me feel very important among the other children. I did not pay much attention to the fact that this money was given to God. To me, the important thing was being the one with the most money to offer.

When I started school, I did not want anybody to know that we were Christians at home. I felt ashamed. Anyway, as I grew up, I had experiences to remind me that God existed.

| Egon and his parents, Ruth and Regner Falk.

RELIGIOUS BONDAGE.

As I grew to become a teenager, I experienced an increasing resistance against the kind of religious life into which I was born.

My "Christian" life had turned into a religious straight jacket. My inward rebellion transformed into a vivid hatred of every Christian I knew—especially my sweet Mum.

My dad often was away from home for weeks when he went out fishing, so my mother had to deal with us on her own most of the time. As a child, I always respected my father profoundly, but I lost my respect for Mother. I turned increasingly nasty and acted very harshly toward her. We had an endless ongoing crisis between us—to the degree that my Mother became very sick. She was unable to handle the situation because of my rebellion and obstinancy. To me, my mother was paramount to religious bondage, and therefore, I vented all my hatred toward Christianity against her. I did not want to live as a Christian, but I was afraid to tell my father.

As a consequence, I experienced crisis upon crisis. I let it all out on my poor mother. Sometimes, I slammed the door closed when I did not want to stay home for another minute. I even scared her by threatening to commit suicide. One night, I once again slammed the door and went for a walk in the darkness. After about one hour, my sister came out searching for me. She told me that Mom was very upset because of my threats to commit suicide, which I was very close to doing. That night, I felt the sinister delight in my power to control her. I did not respect her now that I knew how to exert further pressure on her. At the same time, I felt terrible inside. The main reason for this inner conflict was that my Christian life was nothing but head knowledge, nothing but hearsay. I felt I had never had a personal choice. Christianity had turned into bondage, which I desperately tried to rid myself of.

"CHRISTIANITY" CHANGES TO CHRISTIAN LIFE.

I fought "Christianity" for several years until one autumn night when Daddy was at home with us. We could hear the rain outside, and darkness had come. Mum was quite exhausted because of my attitude as Dad called for me. He said, "Go to your room and get packed. Now, not tomorrow. You leave the house tonight!"

I was 15 years old, and even though I thought I was a grownup, I realized that I had no place to go this autumn night. But I did not want Dad to know this, so I just said, "Well, that´s okay, I´ll leave!"

My feelings threw me into chaos; where could I go? I had nowhere to go, no money, and no food. The fury inside me took over. I had it! I decided to put as much distance between me and "Christianity" as possible. Mum and Dad would now have to realize that I was well able to take care of myself. As I stood there feeling such fury, Dad said, "It's enough, Egon; I have to choose between your mother and you. She is my wife, and you are ruining her. I can't help you. If I have to choose between you two, I have to choose my wife. You will have to manage life on your own from this day on. This is not what I want, but I can't help it. What I really want is for you to be saved—really meet Jesus. But as you don't seem to want this, you better live your own life—on your own and without our help!

READY TO BURST.

I was in turmoil inside, and I was furious. I was very angry with my mother and father, and the hatred clearly showed in my eyes. I would have enjoyed hitting my dad, but he was tall and very strong. I wished I was stronger, so I could beat him up right on the spot. But Dad had mentally and physically the upper hand on me. I had to choose.

My life, my years at home with Mum and Dad—everything passed through my mind. Should I simply leave? Should I try to beat up Dad? Should I just run away? I felt the tears coming.

As I stood there, looking at my dad, something happened; something came over me and broke me down. I found myself kneeling with my dad at my side. He had his big hand on my shoulder, and he started praying for me. I felt the tears bursting forth but wanted to hold them back. I wouldn't allow either Dad or Mom to see my tears. Suddenly, it happened! Everything inside me broke, and the tears spilled from my eyes—I cried and cried. Dad also started crying, and as we were sitting there on the floor, both crying, an atmosphere of love filled the room.

At that moment, when my Dad prayed for me, a miracle took place inside of me: I WAS BORN AGAIN.

I did not understand what was happening, but later, I realized that this was what the Bible tells us about. We can be born again! I really got saved. I had not been saved until that time. The years of childhood and youth had been nothing but a Christian harness as I kept trying to meet God´s demands for me as they were expressed through Mum and Dad. I knew all the Bible stories; I knew how I was expected to live, but I was unable to manage.

BORN AGAIN.

There, in the sitting room of our little house on Bornholm, I was born again. I certainly knew that Jesus had come into my life. I felt how the hatred left me. The bitterness and all the evil in me came out.

I do not remember how long we knelt, but after we had prayed together and wiped away our tears, we got up. Mum was in the kitchen, listening to us. Dad said to me: "Well, if you really have been changed now, then go to your Mum in the kitchen and ask her forgiveness for all the evil you've done to her."

I felt a lump in my throat. It was difficult, but I knew that I had to do it. I went into the kitchen, put my arm around her neck, and said: "Mum, please forgive me for all the evil I've done to you."

That night, we were all crying. Jesus melted us once again,

and there was joy in our home that night. The hatred I had felt for Mum was gone. It left the moment I asked for her forgiveness.

From that time, I realized such joy inside of me. I harmonized with Mum and Dad, and we were doing well in our family.

A NEW DIMENSION OF CHRISTIAN LIFE.

As I continued this way, I knew I was saved and born again, but something was missing. There was too much defeat and too much trouble. I was not succeeding in living my new life the way I was supposed to.

One day, I went to a Youth Conference. I had come to a point of stagnation in my Christian life. I tried to be a witness and live THE NEW LIFE, but I rarely succeeded. It turned out to be mostly defeat.

I felt very disappointed, and one day I told a friend, "This is it! Nobody will ever make me ask for intercession again." He asked me to go with him once more, but I refused. One night after the meeting, he asked me again, but I said, "No, it´s no good; it won´t work for me. From now on, I am just being a usual Christian; there is nothing more for me to get."

He kept on begging me, and one day I accepted his suggestion, but it was not really from my heart. We arrived at the meeting as everyone was praying. The room was packed with praying people, and although we had hoped to sit in the back, we ended up

sitting in the front. Somebody started praying for me, and suddenly, I was completely gone. God´s Holy Spirit came upon me, and I was baptized in the Holy Spirit. I don´t know how long I was gone, but I heard some people singing somewhere far away. I realized what had happened and that only a few people were left in the room, and I spoke a strange language. All I wanted was to keep going, but finally, I, too, had to leave and go home.

After this experience, my spiritual life was changed. Now, I had experienced victory where there once was defeat. I had a real breakthrough in my Christian life. Well, I had been a Christian all the time, but everything had cooled down. Now, after having been baptized in the Holy Spirit, I experienced quite a new dimension.

HANNAH – THE GREATEST GIFT FROM GOD TO ME

Sometime later, we had a Youth Conference 15 miles from my town. The distance kept me from going, although they had meetings every night, and Mum really wanted me to go.

Every morning before leaving for my school and job, Mum said to me, "Tonight you should go, Egon. Lots of young people will be there." She told me about the great meetings they had, the singing, and so on. She wanted me to meet with Jesus and get more from Him, but I did not want to go. Okay, I was a Christian, all right; I just did not feel like going to these meetings.

One morning Mum said to me, "Egon, I was at the meeting last night. Lots of girls were there."

"What did you say?" I asked. "Girls?"

"Yes," she answered. "There were lots of nice girls. I especially noticed two twins last night."

The moment she told me this, I decided to go right from my job to the conference. I was not going just for the meetings; I wanted to take a good look at the girls, especially the twins, and as I saw them, my heart went "boom!"

After the meeting, I tried to get in touch with these twins. I talked to one of them, and the outcome was that I found my dear and sweet wife, Hannah. It was August 1st, 1965. We were tremendously in love with one another. But this was more than falling in love; we had a distinct feeling that God had brought us together. I felt blessed. At the end of the conference, Hannah went back to her home at the other end of Denmark. We didn't see each other for six months, but we exchanged letters and kept in touch.

"The night I met Hannah, God gave me the best gift of my life!" says Egon about his wife.

We got married on July 5th, 1969, and since then, we have served God full-time together and will continue together until the end of our lives.

Hannah has a very strong faith in God, and when I am "down" and want to pack and leave, she is unpacking the very next moment and always tells me to get over it and serve God.

My wife is a very tough lady and always ready to follow me, preaching the Gospel. Together with our small children, Hannah has eaten the most unpleasant food and slept in the most unthinkable places to support me in our ministry.

The first three years in Tanzania were not by any means easy for us all, and through sickness, we were only skin and bones, but even then, Hannah never gave up.

Hannah has been and still is a generous giver, and she is very unselfish in her giving. She is always looking for opportunities for her giving. She has a very big loving heart, and I couldn't live a day without her.

Hannah gave me three wonderful children, Tina, Ruben, and Gitte, and she is a wonderful mom and fantastic grandma.

THE NIGHT I MET HANNAH, GOD GAVE ME THE GREATEST GIFT IN LIFE!

BACK TO THE MBEYA CRUSADE.

I glance at the crowds, grab my Bible, and start preaching the Good News about Jesus.

"Tonight, I am going to tell you about Jesus Christ, the living Son of God. He came to this world as a human being. He was born in Bethlehem in a country called Israel, and they called Him: Friend of Sinners. He healed the sick, delivered the possessed, and forgave the sinners.

Jesus Christ died on a cross because of our sins, but He rose from the dead and lives today! The tomb is empty; Jesus is alive. He promised to be with us every day until the end of the world, and He is here tonight to deliver you from your diseases, from your sins, and from demons. Tonight, you can invite Jesus into your heart. He wants to save and heal you and give you a brand-new life without sin."

The sick people are expectantly watching me. Everyone's eyes are watching this white and buff man who, in the Name of Jesus Christ, is challenging sin, diseases, and evil forces. Tens of thousands of black Africans stand in the square in the darkness while projectors illuminate the platform. The empty mosques are left behind on the horizon, and still more people are closing in to listen.

"If Jesus didn't live, today miracles won't happen in His Name; BUT, IF HE IS ALIVE, YOU WILL SEE HIM DOING MIRACLES HERE TONIGHT!" I continued preaching the Good News. I really believed in what I was saying. I knew for sure from many years of preaching that I was not preaching on my own. Jesus was present to confirm and prove His resurrection from death and His victory over sin, diseases, and demons. I shouted through the large speakers, "Bwana Yesu Asifive!" and the crowds shouted back, "Amina!"

Doubtlessly, I was communicating very well with the immense number of people. I spoke their language and had the contact that it took to make the message reach their hearts. I love Africa, and after so many years in Tanzania, I know the people by heart. These are my people, and I GAVE MY LIFE TO REACH AS MANY AS POSSIBLE FOR HEAVEN.

While I looked over the crowds, my thoughts returned to when I was newly saved and started my preaching ministry. If I had just known then what God had in mind...

BEING A WITNESS FOR JESUS.

I had played around a little on an electric guitar, and I brought my guitar to the church. I accompanied the elderly people as they were singing hymns at the meetings. Not all of them fancied my musical style, but they really did accept and recognize me. I had experiences with God, and I wanted to give Him all I could.

Some of my friends played the organ, bass, and drums, and after a while, we were able to organize the music in meetings. We traveled around for camp meetings, open-air meetings, and so on to testify for Jesus.

Something happened in me as I went out to tell people about Jesus. I knew that this was where I belonged. Maybe part of the evangelist was born during those days, even though no one but God knew about it at the time.

This is why I always tell young people to use whatever they've got for Jesus and begin where they actually are. As Christians, we belong in the place where people are.

At that time, I was alone most of the time. I used to go for long walks, praying and fellowshipping with the Lord. At home in my room, I sensed the presence of God very clearly. I still remember how I was preaching for myself, pretending to hold large meetings in Africa.

Although I was no preacher, the Good News was burning inside me. I wanted to tell the Good News to everybody. As I preached, I saw people before me—Africans! I did not understand what was happening, and I asked myself, "How do I become involved in a ministry like this?" I prayed, "God, please talk to someone in the church; tell them something to confirm that YOU have called me into a full-time ministry as an evangelist."

One Sunday, something happened after a meeting in my church. At the end of the meeting, I was packing up my guitar and amplifier before going home. One of the elders who used to teach the Bible came to me and said, "Egon, please come with me. I feel I have something to tell you from the Lord. God has been speaking to me about you, and last night, I hardly got any sleep because of this. I think God wants me to tell you this: He has called you and wants you to go into a full-time ministry. He will open the doors for you."

I was hit as if God himself spoke to me, for I had never mentioned anything to this elder. It was something just between God and me. As I left church that night, I was on the verge of exploding from joy because God had given me the confirmation I had asked Him for. Now I knew that God wanted me to serve Him full-time.

BEING A LOCAL EVANGELIST.

Soon, I was appointed as a local evangelist in my church. Shortly thereafter, I went to a Bible School course in Copenhagen. I had just finished my studies and training as a qualified mechanical engineer, and my boss had offered me a very good job. At the Bible School, some brothers from a town in Jutland asked me, "When will you come and minister to us? We have no pastor and no preacher." I told them I had to give notice to quit my job before I could go to their church. However, they didn't give up that easily. "Can you start next Wednesday?" This was on Sunday, and I went home to my parents on the island of Bornholm.

They asked me how the Bible course was. I found it quite difficult to tell them that I had to leave to work as an evangelist, but I had already promised the brothers in Jutland that I would come. So, I answered, "Well, I liked it. Wednesday, I have to leave to begin ministering as an evangelist."

"Well," Mum said, "I felt in my heart that someday you would have to go. Are you sure the time has come already?"

But now, nothing could keep me back. The brethren were expecting me, and I had decided to leave Wednesday.

I ministered in that church for a year as an evangelist, and during that time, I polished my preaching, and God helped me through that time, and spiritually, I felt I was growing up. I quickly learned that I don't preach the Gospel to make myself known, but I preach the Gospel to make JESUS known.

Chapter Two
TO NORWAY AND NEW CHALLENGES

After Hannah and I married, we went to Norway in 1970 and lived there for four years. We had now become a family.

We got a place to live and an option to travel around for meetings all over Norway. It was a difficult time. Spiritually, however, it was a very rich period since I was privileged to pray for salvation with an enormous number of people.

Financially, things were very shallow. I often had to leave Hannah and my children without money. At certain times, we did not know what we would eat the following day.

One morning, there was a big cardboard box with a lot of groceries outside our door. We did not know who put it there. In this way, God performed wonders for us and reminded people of our financial situation.

My wife Hannah used to bake our bread since it was cheaper that way.

Once, as I returned from eight weeks of meetings, Hannah was crying in the living room. "Why are you crying?" I asked.

"You know the pot that I keep the flour in?" she answered, "I have been taking flour from it for a long time without looking into it. Now, I need to bake again today, and it does not run out.

There is still flour in the pot even when it should be empty!" She was crying for joy over the goodness of God. We believed and knew God performed a "flour wonder" for us, and this was a wonderful experience. Not only were our physical needs met, but it showed us that God was endorsing our ministry. This was of great importance to us. We were already learning things that later gave us the assurance that God can do what is needed in times of trouble.

These were personal experiences that we kept in our hearts. I remember God giving us a car, but not everybody would agree to an evangelist having a good new car.

In one city, a great church invited me for revival meetings, and upon my arrival, I was received and welcomed by a sister. When she spotted the car, she said, "Is that your car?"

"Yes!" I answered.

"Do you think that you can collect an offering when you are driving a car like that?" she asked.

There is no need to take notice of things like these. We knew in our hearts that we were serving God, and those days were tough many times with no money at all. Sometimes, I didn't even have money for the fare when I was traveling because I was paid so little. But God performed miracles with our finances.

Although I could write a full book just about miracles like these, we keep this book in our hearts. It is our book of remembrance after many years, yes, a lifetime in the service for God.

Chapter Three
PIONEERING IN AFRICA
Culture Shock and Primitive Living.

It was quite a culture shock for all of us. When we attempted to eat breakfast, we had to vomit right away. We could not digest the food, and it was quite challenging for us who came from a country with lovely Danish food and every comfort.

The way we were served there was quite different from back home. On and off, we visited the indigenous people. We came to a hut without water nor electricity. Everyone was seated on the mud floor, and the pots with food were brought in.

One of the most common dishes is a porridge called Ugali, made from ground corn. Everyone eats from the same pot. First, everyone washes his hands in the same brownish water which passes around. As the water is often quite polluted in Africa, you don't exactly feel very clean afterward. Then, you dip your lumps of Ugali into the sauce with your fingers and eat it.

Stuffed bellies of goats or other animals may also be served. It looks like a towel on one side and is not easy to swallow for a Scandinavian. They often have not even properly cleansed the belly because they like the sour taste brought forth by the stomach when the goat or cow has eaten grass. It is not only terrible to eat, but you can smell the stench of the belly on your fingers for several days afterward.

Another dish we might be served in Tanzania is Mlenda. It is a special kind of grass that is slimy and long. When you try to take it out of the pot, it will not let go. It is so tough and slimy that it is possible to pull strings of several feet. You need a special technique to get it out of the pot and to your mouth. It must be drawn up to the pot's edge and then quickly broken off over the edge.

Although this kind of food was very difficult to adjust to, little by little, we managed. We had to get used to it if we were going to live there. In this place where everything was simple and primitive, even the simplest things could be considered wildly luxurious.

We also had to face diseases. We suffered from diarrhea and stomach trouble all the time. Once, I lost almost forty pounds. We were not yet used to the new bacteria flora, so the first time was very tough for all of us. It was a trial for my whole family, but God helped us through.

My biggest hurdle in Africa was the language barrier. I could not preach, and there was nobody who could help me interpret. I had to learn the language, Swahili, which took quite some time.

MY FIRST TASK IN AFRICA.

I could not start as an evangelist, so I had to start with other tasks. I worked as a driver and helped local evangelists. I moved them from village to village, planting new churches.

Once, I moved a family, and my car was full of chickens. The chickens could not stand the hot, dusty, bumpy ride. They died one by one, and we had to throw them out the window. Another time, we had a goat in my car. We tied it inside the car before we went into the hut to pray together and say goodbye. The rope was not long enough for the goat to reach the ground, and there it was, hanging on the verge of suffocation. We barely managed to save its life. There were a lot of similar situations, which for a Scandinavian evangelist were quite inconceivable.

Hannah and I were supporting the local evangelists financially and helped them start and build churches. So, the first period in Africa was a time of learning, where I served as a Jack-of-all-trades and helper for others.

Being a preacher unable to preach was a very strange and frustrating experience. After some months, I was able to make myself understood in Swahili, but it was not until a year later that I could start preaching small sermons.

MY FIRST VENTURE TO THE NATIVES.

After about a year, I went to a neighboring tribe, Barabaig. This was a very fierce tribe. One of the reasons was that the girls didn't want to marry a young man unless he had killed either a lion, an elephant, or another man. Therefore, the girls mocked the young men a lot until they had killed.

These warriors used a spear for the killing. It is not easy to kill a lion or an elephant with a spear, so instead, they killed a lot of people! I had a strong urge to go and proclaim the Good News to this tribe, but it was hard to evoke a sincere desire in any of my fellows to join me. Only one person was willing to join me on this trip. We arranged a permit from the authorities to go to the woods and meet a leader of this tribe.

He understood no Swahili, and it was not easy to communicate, but with "signs and wonders," finally he understood what I wanted. I had an amplifier in my car with a loudspeaker on the roof. The tribal leader was riding with us to tell his people that there would be a meeting.

The mere job of convincing this man to enter my car was a circus. He had never been inside a car before and did not know how to enter it. He tried backward, sideways, and head-on but did not manage to get into it. Finally, we managed to get him in, and he was supposed to hold the microphone in his hand. It was a funny sight! He did not know what a microphone was. We had to explain that the sound of his voice would come out on the roof, but he didn't understand any of this.

We drove around in the car while he was speaking, but I didn't understand what he said. Finally, we stopped at the big tree where the meeting was supposed to be. Little by little, people came out of the bush and sat down neatly in the shade of the big tree. This was the tree where all the important meetings for the tribe were held. There were approximately a hundred people or so waiting for me to speak.

I did not speak their language, and they knew no Swahili. But there was a young man who had gone to school and knew Swahili. He was supposed to interpret for me. He was not a Christian, so it seemed hopeless. He could say whatever he wanted, and I had no way of controlling it. But the Name of Jesus is quite alike in any language, so I kept on repeating it every so often to hear if he was saying the same thing. When I had finished preaching, I asked if anyone would like to receive Jesus and be saved, but not a person came forth. Everyone simply remained seated while staring at me. I was completely downcast.

As we drove back home, I was very discouraged that I could not reach these people with the Good News. I felt that everything was hopeless. But I felt that I had to go back again to try once more.

As we tried to go back sometime later, a tribal war broke out, and they threw stones at my car and attacked us. It was impossible to get through, and we had to leave.

After several years I was having a seminar for ministers in a neighboring tribe. On impulse, I asked, "Is there anyone present from the Barabaig tribe?"

In 1974, Hannah and Egon traveled to Africa as missionaries. Here is a long-haired Egon along with members of the dangerous Barabaig tribe, whom they tried to reach with the Christian message.

Suddenly, a young man jumped up and said, "I am from the Barabaig tribe!"

"How were you saved?" I asked. It turned out that during the meeting under the big tree many years ago, when no one expressed any desire to be saved, the Word of God had been

sewed into the heart of this young man, and shortly thereafter, he was saved.

Today, many members of this tribe serve God and have planted many churches. The culture is totally changed, and no killing is taking place anymore.

The Barabaig girls mocked the young men until they had shown they could kill a lion, an elephant - or another man ..

In that first meeting under the big tree in which I felt I had failed, God started a mighty work among the people of Barabaig. So, despite the small beginning with language barriers and cultural differences, the Good News had the dynamic power to penetrate.

THE BEGINNING OF A NEW ERA.

In 1983, we added a new ministry to our mission work. Again, it was a small beginning, complicated in so many ways. But, after a while, we realized that our love for the people gave us the power and courage to continue.

We started a school ministry and traveled to different schools, colleges, and universities all over the country.

In one school, several hundreds of students came to hear the Good News. After my preaching, I gave an invitation to receive Christ Jesus as their Savior and Lord, and more than two hundred stood up on their chairs ready to receive. I was almost shocked and thought that they might have misunderstood me, so I said, "Sit down again!" Then, I started all over and explained what it meant to become a Christian. I gave a thorough lecture on that.

I asked again, "You, who want to receive Jesus and be saved and born again, stand on your chair." Now, more than two hundred young students were standing up and praying the sinner's prayer together with me.

Everywhere we went, hundreds of young people repented and received the Lord Jesus. This mission to schools became our main ministry for several years, and we went from town to town to proclaim the Good News of Jesus.

Barabaig fights with a spear that could easily pierce an enemy.

Chapter Four
CRUSADES
The birth of new life outreach

While we were visiting the schools, I felt that we had to reach further out to the people—the whole Nation.

I began to organize crusades for invited evangelists. I was a bit afraid to stand on the platform in such big open-air meetings. However, after a while, I felt a stronger and stronger fire in my heart. This was where I belonged, on the platform in large crusades with thousands of people, impacting the whole community. Here, I was at home. The time had come to let loose the evangelist within me to proclaim the Good News as I had seen in the vision God had shown me back on Bornholm when I was newly saved.

It was another small beginning. I had bought two small loudspeakers, but I didn't have a platform at that time. However, the blessing of God was upon the things I did, and many were saved in these open-air meetings. This was the beginning of the ministry we are in today. New Life Outreach was born.

Little by little, we managed to buy more equipment, even a larger trailer. We were planning to buy a bigger truck in Denmark, but at that time, Reinhard Bonnke had started his large crusades in Africa. He needed new equipment, and we were offered to buy one of his 18-wheelers. It was a big 18-wheeler with two big shipping containers on it, but God had given us faith in our hearts, and we saw a vision of winning a lot of people for God in Tanzania.

Besides this, we had terrible living conditions as we traveled for open air-meetings. Sometimes, we might sleep in a vacant room in a church or in a guest house which might be dirty, with people drinking and carousing all night. In the long run, it was unbearable. Living under such primitive conditions was a burden, and it was very hard to keep spiritually strong during the crusades.

I often traveled alone with my African team while my wife Hannah stayed back home. Once, I noticed that all the team members slept in their cars, and I asked them why. They told me they couldn't sleep in the room because of all the rats. So,

when the Africans themselves couldn't bear the living conditions, you probably understand why this was not acceptable in the long run.

By God's grace and mercy, we got a second 18-wheeler and built our accommodations in the shipping containers, and it was nice and safe.

These accommodations protected us from wild animals, robbers, and others who might want to harm or kill us. Dangers are lurking everywhere, and when the people see the white evangelist with a lot of equipment, some of them see an opportunity to rob us.

I learned and experienced that the higher the goal we set, the more God intervened and helped us during the ministry we did.

Chapter Five
SIGNS, WONDERS, AND HEALINGS

"Tonight, you can meet Jesus where you are. He will save and heal you and give you a brand-new life without sin."

We are back in Mbeya again, where this story started.

Now the time had come in the meeting when I set into the deep waters in my preaching. I proclaim the living Jesus, who is able to heal the sick today!

"If Jesus isn't alive today, there can be no wonders in His Name. BUT IF HE LIVES, YOU SHALL SEE HIS WORKS HERE TONIGHT!" I went on proclaiming the Good News with a strong faith in what I was saying. I knew after many years in the ministry that I was not alone in my faith proclamation. Jesus himself was present to confirm and prove His resurrection from the dead and His power over sin, disease, and demons.

Suddenly, there was movement in the sea of people. What was happening now? Many people were rejoicing as a group of people approached the platform. You could see only two crutches stretched upward. A man emerged from this monstrous mass of people onto the platform.

This man was a cripple when he came to the meeting, his

family testified, but now he was completely healed. When the big crowd recognized what just happened, everyone broke out, rejoicing, jumping and dancing and waving with whatever they had in their hands. Many of those who knew this gentleman and knew that he had been completely crippled hardly believed their own eyes.

The man walked back and forth on my platform with tears running down his cheeks in thanks to Jesus. He saw his legs completely healed. He could walk!

THE BREAKTHROUGH IN THE MEETING HAD COME!

THIS WAS THE MOMENT I HAD BEEN WAITING FOR.

THE PROOF THAT THE GOOD NEWS IS TRUE HAD NOW APPEARED BEFORE THE EYES OF EVERYONE.

All the time I had been preaching, I had known that Jesus was present. But I also knew that I am powerless in my own strength when it comes to healing. Only Jesus can perform wonders.

It was now happening again and again. A new atmosphere seized the crowd. An invisible power was present. Everyone felt it, and everyone knew that more people could be healed. The atmosphere was flooded with FAITH IN JESUS. For me, this was the very MOMENT that I had been waiting for. As a fisherman waits for the net to fill before he pulls it aboard, my team and I had been waiting for this MOMENT.

I took my microphone and said, "Jesus has begun healing the sick tonight. Expect your miracle here and now!"

For the bystanders, it was completely beyond their grasp. The things which took place before their eyes were the same as had happened in the first church. Read Acts 5:15-16.

As the meeting in Mbeya continued, I began to speak, "Many Christians today are preoccupied with signs and wonders for the sake of signs and wonders. In the Western World, they want to see signs and wonders, often as a kind of entertainment during the meetings.

In Africa, the signs and wonders will often be decisive as to whether the Good News will break through in a town or not. In Africa, people are spiritually focused. They believe in spirits, with every village having its own witch doctor, whom they consult whenever they are having difficulties. The witch doctor will conjure up the spirits over the people and give them recipes and formulas, which are meant to protect them against evil spirits and heal them. These witch doctors are revered in their local societies, and they will attempt to fight anything that threatens their position.

Egon Falk gathers walking sticks from healed Africans.

In another crusade, another man, who also was totally crippled, told the crowds that he had used all his money to pay the witch doctors. He had been forced to sell his business to raise enough money. Yet, he was getting worse and worse. In my meeting, he was completely healed, and he came to the microphone to tell his story to everyone. At the end, he said, "Today, Jesus has not only healed me but also saved me!"

I have always proclaimed the Good News of Jesus Christ, never faith or healing—only Jesus! But, when they began to bring their sick people to my meetings, I met a new and important challenge. The Bible tells us that Jesus healed all manner of disease and feebleness. The first Christians experienced signs, wonders, and healings in their ministry. What should I do with the sick who came to my meetings? I had to pray for them!

A NEW THING HAPPENED AS WE BEGAN THE CRUSADES.

I have always prayed for the sick, ever since we arrived and began our ministries in Africa, and before that, also in Europe.

But everything became stronger when we started the crusades. I suddenly found myself amidst lots of sick people. They brought along lame, cripples, and people with all kinds of diseases and wanted me to pray for them all. When the first healings took place, faith was ignited in our hearts. The Acts of power were new to us at that time, but today it is quite normal. We have come to know God as the healer of the sick people.

We have many memories and experiences of how God has changed people and healed them. This has been a great encouragement for us in the work for the Kingdom of God, and it has taught us a lot.

HEALED FROM CHRONIC MALARIA.

In one meeting, a lawyer whom I did not know was present. This lawyer was in a meeting where he saw the sick being healed. He had a sick daughter at home who had been bound for two years, suffering from chronic malaria. The healings he saw really impressed him.

After this meeting, he went back to his home in Arusha. One day, a pastor came into his office, and as he said hello to him, the lawyer asked, "Are you familiar with Dr. Egon Falk?"

"Sure!" the pastor responded. "He is one of my good friends."
"Can you put me in touch with him?" the lawyer asked. "I have a daughter who has been suffering from chronic malaria for almost two years."

I was asked to visit this family to pray for their daughter. When I arrived, I realized that his wife was a judge in Arusha. The lawyer said to me, "I saw what Jesus did in the crusade you held. Can you now pray for my daughter?"

I prayed for his daughter, and after a while, I left the place. Sometime later, I met the lawyer and asked, "How is your daughter doing?"

"She is better now," he answered. Every time I met him, he told me that she was better. Once, as I was driving down the street, I suddenly saw her walking in the street. I stopped and talked to her. She told me that she was now completely well. Her father had been to a meeting and received faith for his daughter's healing.

The testimonies from all the people—and they are many—who are healed are the best advertisements we might possibly get for our meetings.

A PERSON DYING FROM CANCER IS HEALED.

In Morogoro, a city with a great number of Muslims, a powerful thing took place during one of my crusades. Suddenly, without my noticing, a lady who was dying of cancer was placed on my platform. While I was preaching, some family members put her there for me to pray for her. At the end of the meeting, I prayed for the sick and knew she was lying there, waiting for me to pray for her. I prayed for a long time, and finally, I shouted, "Amen!" As I turned to walk away, I heard the crowd going wild. They yelled and screamed.

I thought, "What's going on now?" I saw that the woman who had been lying lifeless on my platform was running after me. The power of God had come upon her and healed her. She now jumped around and praised God. I asked her who she was and why she was in my meeting. She told me that her sisters had brought her to the meeting, and I called them both to the platform. They came and confirmed that they had driven their sister to the meeting. She had been hospitalized with cancer for a year at the Muhimbilli Hospital in Dar Es Salaam, the biggest and leading hospital in Tanzania. She had recently been returned home to Morogoro to die. She was unable to stand on her own; she was dying from cancer. This woman was saved and healed that night. It was a powerful experience for us all.

HEALED FROM CHILDLESSNESS.

In 1989, we held a crusade in a town called Mwanza. As our team came back two years later to plan another crusade, they met a little boy named Egon. Typically, no one in Tanzania is called Egon, as they don´t know how to pronounce it. It is really difficult to say Egon in Swahili. Otherwise, it is quite common to call children after events or persons. It turned out that the parents of this little fellow had been to the meetings two years earlier. They had been barren and had no children. This is considered a great shame in the African culture and is almost considered a curse. The husband has some kind of right to expel his wife if she cannot give birth to a baby. Earlier, they had consulted many witch doctors, and during these occult rituals, she had been possessed by demons. In my meeting, they had been saved and delivered from the demonic powers which had governed their lives. It was only a few months after the meetings that the woman became pregnant. She gave birth to a healthy baby boy, and therefore, she said, "This is God´s answer to prayer. It is a result of Dr. Egon´s crusade, and therefore, he shall be called Egon."

This boy, who by now is an adult, is living evidence of the fact that Jesus performs miracles today. Wherever his name—Egon—is mentioned, they tell the story of how he was born.

A DEAF MUTE IS HEALED.

In a Muslim town called Iganga, Uganda, we had another crusade.

A deaf and mute elderly man was healed in one of my meetings. He came to the meeting together with his brothers.

As they returned home Saturday night after the meeting, they discovered that he now could hear. It was a great miracle for all of them. However, he still could not speak. Sunday morning, they returned to the church meeting. They brought their brother to me at the platform and said that he had been healed from deafness the night before. As I examined him, I found that he really could hear everything clearly. We prayed for him in the name of Jesus. After that, I wanted to see if he was now able to speak. A deaf-mute can't say a word since he has never heard one. I tried to teach him a sentence. In Uganda, they speak English or a tribal language. I told him to repeat after me, saying, "I love Jesus." Suddenly, this elderly gentleman, loud and clear, responded in English, "I love Jesus!"

People went completely crazy. We brought him to the crusade meeting that night, and people who knew him had heard what God had done in the church service. They now came to the crusade meeting to see and listen to him. I brought him to the platform, and he repeated again and again, "I LOVE JESUS!"

We could hardly control the crowds since people were so happy and excited.

After the meeting, the leading Muslim Iman came to me and said, "I am so happy that you leave town tomorrow."

"Why?" I asked.

"Because there is nobody left in my mosque," he answered. "They have all gone to your crusade meetings, so I might as well leave town."

A happy Muslim man tests his healing after intercession.

Chapter Six

THE THINGS WHICH ARE SEEN WERE NOT MADE OF THINGS WHICH ARE VISIBLE

By Pastor Frede Rasmussen

One afternoon in 1993, a few hours before the afternoon meeting of the crusade, Egon Falk and I were sitting in his RV trailer in the town of Geita near Lake Victoria.

We had had lunch with the worship team and were now alone in the trailer, sharing life and faith. Egon put a cassette on his cassette player, and we both became deeply engrossed in the testimony of Gunnar Olsson, a Swedish businessman who traveled the world, encouraging business people to believe that God is still a miracle-working God.

Frede Rasmussen was pastor at Citykirken in Aarhus, Denmark from 1977 - 2008.

On the tape, Olsson shared remarkable testimonies of how God had miraculously revived businesses, healed people, and mended marriages through his ministry.

We were moved to tears, listening to what God is able to do, and we had a strong sense of God's presence and power on that afternoon on Lake Victoria. But let me start at the beginning...

Egon and I have known each other since our ministries' early beginnings in the Kingdom of God. Egon traveled throughout Scandinavia, mostly in Norway and Denmark, and ministered the gospel, preaching and singing. At that same time, my wife and I were planting a church on Denmark's west coast. In 1974, Hannah and Egon moved to Tanzania, where I visited them for the first time in 1976. One year later, Hannah and Egon took over the church plant when my wife and I moved to the second largest town in Denmark, Aarhus. In the following years, Egon would travel to Tanzania every summer and stay for several weeks, preaching the gospel. During these extended stays, Egon's visions for founding a work in Tanzania were fueled. In 1983, Hannah and Egon moved back to Africa, where they laid the foundation for their present work, New Life Outreach (NLO). One of the cornerstones of their work was Reinhard Bonnke's donation of crusade equipment, including trucks, a platform, and sound equipment, making it possible for them to reach thousands of people wherever they went on gospel crusades and outreaches. It has been amazing to follow this work's growth during the past 37 years in Arusha in northern Tanzania. The church that my wife and I pastored in Aarhus has been involved for many years, so we have closely followed the work in Arusha. Numerous times have we traveled to Arusha and been a part of the crusades throughout Tanzania. The crusades held all over Tanzania have always been the heart and soul of Egon Falk's ministry. Through the crusades, Egon connects with people and churches all over the nation. With the help and support from churches in the US, Egon and Hannah further expanded NLO with a conference center and auditorium to facilitate the hundreds of people who were met by God and came to faith at the crusades. These new Christians came from all corners of Tanzania and were confirmed in their calling and equipped for ministry at the center.

At the beginning of the nineties, our friendship was deepened when Ruben Falk, Hannah and Egon's son, came to our town of Aarhus to begin his studies. He later went to a Bible school in Sweden, and when he came back to Aarhus, he married our daughter, Hanne. Shortly after the wedding, they moved to Tanzania to join the work, which just kept growing. Ruben became the general manager responsible for the crusades' practical aspects, with Arusha as the center for maintaining the vehicles and a growing staff.

Ruben, Hanne, and their baby daughter joined Hannah and Egon at the crusades, where multitudes received Jesus as their Savior, deliverer, and healer, which led to establishing a Bible school, which had its beginning in a few offices. But the Bible school kept growing and had to be moved to the big conference auditorium. NLO also established a local church, which uses the conference auditorium for Sunday services.

Every time we visited Hannah and Egon, Hanne, Ruben, and our granddaughter, we enjoyed seeing how the work grew and progressed. Many volunteers from Europe and the U.S. came to Arusha to join the ministry—and in the middle of this, Ruben and Hanne started a Kindergarten.

Land was purchased, and a shed was built and painted yellow. The Kindergarten started with 20-25 children and quickly became a success because the children of Tanzania are the nation's future and hope. It was not long before NLO had to acquire a much larger piece of land with more space for future buildings.

With funds from churches in Denmark, donations from a denomination in Finland and the Finnish State, among others, buildings for classrooms, cafeteria and kitchen, computer and physics labs, soccer fields, and student housing were built. In one corner, an orphanage for 25 girls was built. The building was named "Hailey's House," and the orphaned girls can grow up safely here. Seeing all the activity, the hustle and bustle of the grounds makes me very thankful, and it is impressive.

In the local community of Olosiva, where the school is located, NLO launched a well project, funded by Danish sponsors, to provide water for the community.

The need to expand the Bible school continued to grow, and yet another piece of land just behind Hannah and Egon's private home was purchased. Several buildings have been built with rooms for 100 Bible school students who have traveled far to study the Bible and be equipped to bring the gospel back out to the people of Tanzania.

Having regularly visited Hannah and Egon, following their life's work, and having watched the life and growth of their ministry throughout the years, I am filled with joy, excitement, thankfulness, and admiration at what God can do through people who make themselves available to Him and His calling. This ministry is an enormous miracle that has emerged over a relatively short time in Tanzania. Through it all, Egon Falk has been faithful to the vision that God has laid upon his heart. The God-given dream in Egon's heart has become a reality before our eyes. This ministry is concrete evidence of what God can do through people who make themselves available to Him. However, there is yet another side to Egon Falk's ministry.

Having traveled with Egon in Africa on crusades and campaigns, my mind is flooded with many memories, impressions, and images—and I would like to share a few with you.

Driving on extremely bad roads, which brutally tested our equipment and vehicles, we had to stop at the nearest mechanic. While repairing our tire, the mechanic told us how he had come to believe in Jesus at one of Egon's crusades in a nearby town. On another occasion, we drove around in a safari park, and a safari jeep full of tourists approached us. The African chauffeur recognized Egon, stopped the Jeep, and began telling us how he had met and received Jesus as his savior in one of Egon's crusades. This happened all the time.

Many miracles happened at every single crusade. I especially remember a crusade far from Arusha. A man had left early in the morning with his sick wife because she wanted to be healed from her crippling disease. With his wife on the back of his bicycle, the man bicycled all day. The meeting had long since begun when they arrived in the town where the crusade was held. That evening became their evening because the wife was healed and jumped around on the platform, praising God for His miraculous intervention. This must have been what Peter and John experienced at the Beautiful Gate when a paralyzed man was healed and began walking, leaping, and praising God.

At the crusades across Tanzania, all denominations gather to support the meetings. In the mornings, hundreds of Christians gather in the largest church to listen to the word of God. The Spirit of God is at work, and people feel the presence of the Spirit as they sing praises to the living God. Participating in such a gathering, full of joyous shouting and dancing in the presence of God, is quite an experience to a pastor who is used to the reserved distance of Scandinavians. And it is quite an experience when thousands of possessed people are delivered from demons at the altar. Or when witch doctors turn from demons and surrender to Christ and a new life and throw all their paraphernalia on the platform to begin a new life with Christ.

To have seen, experienced, and been a small part of all this has been a privilege and enrichment to my wife and me. It has been a joy to have been invited to dedications of buildings, schools, and auditoriums, to Christmas celebrations for coworkers in NLO, to graduation celebrations for Bible school students in their robes and tasseled square graduate hats in crowded auditoriums, to the dedication of the Secondary School with a full day's celebrations and a large choir in colorful robes.

All of these memories point to God, who one day called a young man from a small island in Denmark to a ministry in His vineyard.

May God's blessings continue to rest on Hannah and Egon's ministry in Tanzania.

A witch doctor burns his occult remedies after accepting Jesus Christ as Savior and Lord in his life.

Chapter Seven
CONFRONTATIONS AND RIOTS

We were back in Mbeya again, where I continued the meetings in this enormous crusade. Immense crowds had gathered in the stadium because the rumors had spread all over town of the white man who healed the sick and brought along an unknown power.

My team and I were unaware of the fact that some witch doctors had heard more than enough about this man with the power of God.

Their passion was threatened. If they did nothing about it, this man and this Jesus whom he proclaimed would be the strongest power in town. They decided to stop it with their powers.

There was a rumor that the white man had said that all the charms and amulets people had received from the witch doctors would be burned at the Sunday night meeting.

They came to the meeting and saw the big crowd excited and rejoicing. I noticed some men whom I understood to be witch doctors approaching the platform.

This happened while people were coming to the platform to testify of what Jesus had done for them.

Suddenly, one of the younger men entered my platform by

force. I looked at him and thought, "What now?" I prayed a silent prayer within me, "Dear Jesus, manifest your power, so that everyone will see that you are the strongest and that you have power over the evil spirits."

The young man grabbed the microphone and began to mock Jesus and tried to make the people laugh. He tried to ridicule the whole meeting.

I had to stop him, which I did, and in the same moment as he climbed down the platform, an invisible power grabbed ahold of him, and he was dumbfounded by it. He became confused and began running around. Momentarily, he had lost his mind completely and acted totally insane.

The whole crowd watched what happened and continued to rejoice and praise Jesus. Now they saw who represented the strongest power in town. The witch doctors had to retire in fear due to what happened to this man, who was one of their own.

I simply watched it all, and I have had so many experiences where the witch doctors have had to yield to the power of the name of Jesus.

THE WITCH DOCTOR OF TANGA, WHO RECEIVED CHRIST JESUS.

One night in a crusade, a man came forward for prayer to receive Christ. I could not see that he was actually a witch doctor because he was dressed like any other person. The following day, he came around and said, "Everyone in this town knows me. I am a famous witch doctor. I have been performing sorcery for many years. But now, I have received Jesus, and I want you to burn the potions and paraphernalia which I have used when ministering to my clients."

"I would like to see what you have before we burn it!" I said. As the former witch doctor brought forth the things, the native pastors stopped me. "Egon, please don´t touch that stuff; you may die from it!" they said.

"No! He who is in me is greater than he who is in these things!" I said.

I looked into the box, which contained bird feathers, animal horns, a book with strange symbols and words, and many other odd items.

I said, "I would like to exhibit these things at the soccer stadium tonight. Can you agree with that?"

"That is okay!" he said.

At the evening meeting, I brought all his gear and showed it to the crowds, and they hollered and screamed, "Don't touch it, white man! It is dangerous; you will die!"

But I brought one thing forth after another, saying, "Jesus is our Savior. He has saved the sorcerer. These things can do no harm." Then we burned it all in the fire.

After a couple of years, I returned to Tanga for a new crusade. The sorcerer, whom I remembered from the former meeting, came up to me. Across the chest of his T-shirt, I read the word: "Counselor."

As I stood there, watching this former sorcerer who had now become an active member of the church, it was a strong testimony to the fact that Jesus can save anyone. His power is so much stronger than that of the entire crowd of occultists put together.

When I see sorcerers come to my meetings to destroy, I know that Jesus will transform them also so that they will be saved and get a new life.

IDOL WORSHIPPERS ATTEMPTING AN ATTACK.

While I still was thinking of the sorcerer from Tanga, another thing happened in a crusade in Nairobi, Kenya's capital.

An African had climbed the sound tower to throw down our equipment. I saw something happening over there, but I couldn't see exactly what was going on. Could it be the idol worshippers that the police warned me about yesterday? The police had told me yesterday that a group of idol worshippers who worship the god of Mount Kenya planned to kill me.

I continued to communicate with the crowds while I was watching the man in the sound tower. Hundreds of questions raced through my head. Will they attack? Has the devil sent this group to kill me? Where are the police? They had promised to post hundreds of civil policemen in the crowd in case this group tried to strike. But where were they? I tried to keep calm, but sweat started to run down my brow. I knew that it could be dangerous if they attacked. How could the police possibly stop them in the dark in this big crowd of people?

Suddenly, two cars drove up to the P.A. towers and stopped, facing me. Several Africans in traditional sheepskin clothes jumped out and stared at me. They brought out knives, clubs, and different kinds of traditional weapons. I wanted to stop my preaching, even I was struggling.

Unless the police appeared right away, I had to take precautions for my team's and the crowd's safety. Seconds felt like hours.

What now? Where are the police? People started to climb up the sound tower to destroy our equipment and stop the meeting.

I had a hard time concentrating on my preaching, but I knew that I was the only one to "control" the meeting to avoid panic.

Suddenly, a gang of the idol-worshippers appeared close to my platform, and I heard them say, "He is the one we have come to kill!" At that moment, I sensed the power of the Holy Spirit descending upon not only me but all over the place. It was like an invisible mantle covering all of us. I went on preaching with extra power fire without looking at those who had come to kill me.

I offered a short silent prayer within me, "Dear Jesus, intervene now; save them!" Within a few minutes, many idol worshipers came forth and stood near the platform. They didn't do anything but listen to what I was preaching. They seemed completely paralyzed where they stood. They didn't even make a move. It looked like an invisible power kept them in check.

What looked like a dangerous situation had, for a moment, been calmed.

I recognized the peace which spread upon the crowd. I became calmer and continued to preach full speed, "You who want to become a Christian here tonight, come forward and receive Jesus!"

I was in an important phase of the meeting now when I invite people to be saved.

GOD IS IN CONTROL.

God has held his protecting hands above us in many dangerous situations and for many years.

In 1992, in Bukoba, in the northwestern part of Tanzania, God really saved us from another perilous situation.

I had permission to do a crusade at the very best square in town. But it was situated right opposite a Muslim mosque. At that time, a group of Muslims threatened to pour barrels of gasoline over the platform and all the equipment and burn it down. They even threatened to pour hundreds of gallons of gasoline over the people if I began preaching.

Just before the crusade meeting started, the secret police ordered everybody to come to their office because some radical Muslims were planning to make trouble.

I was asked to move and rebuild the platform and all the equipment, so the Muslims could see that the Christians were not out to provoke or make trouble.

It was a big job to take down our platform and equipment and rebuild at another spot in Bukoba town, but we did it, and hundreds of Christians came and helped us; even the police and military personal gave us a hand. Everyone was jumping and dancing in the streets of Bukoba as they moved our equipment. It was a victory march!

The radical Muslims and the devil didn't recognize the kind of advertisement this was giving us. The rumor went not only all over town but spread like wildfire to the whole area.

The next day, when we opened the crusade, we met tens of thousands of people who were ready to receive the Gospel of Jesus Christ.

The chief of police, authorities, politicians—they were all present.

The crusade turned out to be a mighty victory for the Kingdom of God, and thousands were saved.

DEMON POSSESSED MAN DELIVERED.

Suddenly, something happened in another meeting. Yelling and howling are heard in front of my platform. We see several people waving their arms in an attempt to escape. Then I see what is causing it. A young man is crawling on all fours, barking like a wild and crazy dog. Foam is running from his mouth as he attempts to bite all who are near him, and people are scared and trying to escape.

Several of my team members arrive at the scene. They have been trained to handle the demon-possessed in my crusades. They grab this young man and bring him behind my platform, where there is a fenced-in area used to pray for these people. I went down to him, and the man attempted to bite me just like an angry, crazy dog. "In the mighty Name of Jesus, come out of him, you devil!"

Yes, I am used to it and have done it thousands of times. I know for sure there is Heavenly Power in the Mighty Name of Jesus.

Suddenly, the eyes of the young man roll violently, and his whole body shakes. Then, he seemingly has a complete blackout. He has absolutely no sense of what is going on around him. This goes on for some minutes; then, he falls to the ground as if completely lifeless. Then after a few minutes, he "wakes up," looking around as if he does not know where he is. Now, he looks quite normal, the foam around his mouth is gone, and he is silent. He is delivered!

Demon possession is very common in Africa. Everybody believes in evil spirits and the spiritual world, and everyone knows there is a God and a devil.

Often, while I am preaching, and certainly when we begin praying, we witness people falling or beginning to shake all over. Sometimes, we have to bind their arms and legs with rope to prevent them from hurting themselves or others. Demons can be very strong and violent.

They vomit and scream. It's like going to Hell.

Typically, they become some kind of unconscious, so they don't know what is going on when the Spirit of God comes upon them. When they are delivered, they wake up and ask, "What has happened?" Then we tell them, you have been delivered from evil spirits—Jesus has set you free. Now, you need to receive Jesus as your Lord and Savior and have your sins forgiven!"

When they are filled with the Holy Spirit, it is wonderful to note the difference. Those who were a few minutes ago raving mad are now completely transformed.

Some people think that these phenomena occur only in third-world cultures. But evil spirits are at work in Western cultures as well.

BACK TO MBEYA.

The Gospel of Jesus has been preached and proclaimed. I challenge every person to repent and believe in Jesus as their Lord and Savior. I go right to the point and say, "YOU, who want to repent from all of your sins and believe in Jesus, come NOW forward to the platform."

Now, it's time to pull in the net, and the devil shall NOT have the victory!

Several thousands of people gush forward to receive Jesus as we are singing "YESU NAMBA MOJA" - Jesus is number one!

These crusade meetings are a far cry from meetings in the Western world as the Africans by the thousands begin waving branches, handkerchiefs, and dancing while they sing to Jesus.

One thing is for sure, thousands of people receive Jesus for the very first time this night in Mbeya.

JESUS IS HARVESTING NATIONS FROM ALL OVER THE WORLD LIKE HE SAID: "THE HARVEST IS THE END OF THIS AGE."

This is the very moment my wife Hannah and I live for. This is what we have given our lives for.

All the striving sweat and controversies through so many years are swallowed up in a genuine proclamation of victory in which the whole area of Mbeya is experiencing THE POWER OF GOD UNTO SALVATION.

OUR HOME AWAY FROM HOME.

After the crusade meeting, we retire to our "home," an 18-wheeler with two steel shipping containers. Some barred windows and a stairway to the door are the only visible signs that this is not just another ordinary shipping container. It's completely dark outside.

The only audible sounds are the humming of thousands of insects swarming in the darkness. From a distance, the sound of howling is heard—probably wild dogs. A quick glance upward presents a starry sky, which is quite breathtaking.

This humid and hot air, the smell—yes, this is Africa indeed.

Luxury and modern facilities are so nonexistent that the life we used to live in the Western world seems like a dream.

When you enter our "living room," it reminds you of any camper except for the barred windows.

One of our many minister/pastor visitors put it like this. "The contrast between the strong supernatural ministry in which Dr. Egon and Hannah are, and their natural simplicity is striking. Often, we may have an idea that people whom God uses in such

a special way are not 'ordinary' people. Quite a number of the servants of God have been caught up in their own success. They are surrounded by luxury, ride private planes, and live in expensive hotels. Dr. Egon and Hannah Falk's life and service contradict the claims that all preachers God uses in especially mighty ways have to puff up and remove themselves from the man in the street. They are plain and natural in their private life, but signs and wonders are part of their everyday life in Tanzania."

That evening, talking to our visitor, I tell him that miracles, signs, and wonders are no goal *per se*. The real purpose is for people to see that Jesus is really alive. What we experience here is nothing more than what we read in the Bible. (James 5:17-18) When he prayed that it might not rain, there was no rain for three and a half years. Then he prayed again for the heavens to release their rain for the earth to bear fruit again.

Without signs and wonders, we are completely powerless in our ministry in Africa.

We need to come as Paul expressed it in 1. Cor. 2:4 *"With a demonstration of the power of the spirit."* People in Africa are used to powerful works through the sorcerers and witch doctors. If the God that we proclaim cannot prove his existence through signs, wonders, and spiritual power, we cannot reach the people and make them believe.

As we continue drinking our strong African coffee with Danish cookies made by my dear wife Hannah, I express to my friend from Europe that it never begins on the big platform in the large crusade meeting. All of us must be willing to lay our lives completely into the hands of God and go all the way—from the small talks to the bigger.

Those who have reached furthest into the Kingdom of God, those who have suffered adversities and trial, served faithfully in the small beginnings, can remain humble when God allows signs, wonders, and miracles.

Such a life with God is an exciting life. There are no boring periods, but it is a life filled with continual experiences of the power of God.

Our cozy evening with our friend is coming to an end, and as we are praying together, it feels like God is ever so close.

Time has passed quickly during this crusade. All the trucks and 18-wheelers with all the equipment are ready to leave for another crusade.

As we are leaving town, people wave from every direction. Everybody in town now has heard the Good News about Jesus, our Savior and Lord.

Another crusade is finished, and Jesus has harvested thousands of precious people who now are destined to Heaven. How many exactly, He knows.

The moment we leave the town, something happens. A strong wind suddenly starts blowing, and clouds gather, heavy and dark. Suddenly, it seems like the heavens are bursting all around, and rain pours down all over town. Now, it's raining on the soccer stadium for the first time in months.

Dr. Egon turns around, looking at the heavy rain, and says to his visitor friend, "Didn't I tell you?" A broad smile appears on his face.

Some young ministers asked me about the greatest miracle I ever had seen and experienced. I had to pause and think for a minute because every miracle for the person who receives it is a great miracle.

Some miracles can't be seen with your physical eyes. If you are in terrible pain, you feel it, but not your neighbor or friend, and when you are healed, YOU know you are healed!

Chapter Eight
WHAT IS A MIRACLE?

It's a great event that you, by faith and prayers, can prepare for and expect to happen according to God's Word. According to Jesus in Mark 9:23, everything is possible for him who believes.

Secondly, it's something you can't do but only God.

Thirdly, a true miracle will always point to HIM who did it and bring Glory to God.

People can experience great miracles and still lose their lives and end up in Hell.

I truly believe the greatest miracle is receiving forgiveness from our sins, being saved and born again, being a NEW creation in Christ; the old has gone, the NEW has come! 2. Corinthians 5:17

Followers of Jesus can have a physical handicap and still go to Heaven, and on the resurrection day, they will be resurrected without their handicaps—all will be healed. THAT'S A MIRACLE!

I was born into a professional fisherman's family on the island of Bornholm, Denmark, in the small village of Tejn.

I remember several times when my mother Ruth called me, my sister, and my little brother into the living room for prayers. The weather was stormy and very bad; we knelt and prayed for Dad and his workers to be safe and return home without any harm from the angry ocean.

Often, fear wanted to take control over my mind when I looked at the colossal waves pounding the big rocks close to our house. Dad was out there somewhere, and I knew several fishermen who never made it home. I wanted my Dad safely home, and as a little child, I learned to pray and trust God for miracles.

When I was 14 years old, I began having pain in my right hip and finally wasn't able to walk at all. I remember the cold and dark winter morning when the ambulance came and took me to the hospital.

I was totally bedbound, and even a bathroom visit was impossible for me. It wasn't fun at all for a 14-year-young boy. The doctors did the best they could but still no healing at all. I was devastated when I was told I would be bound to the bed for a long time.

One day, our church pastor came to visit me, and even as shy as I was, I allowed him to pray for me and anoint me with oil, according to James 5:14. There were five other men in the same room with me; they looked strangely at me, and they didn't understand what was going on.

That following night, something strange happened. The only thing I remember was the nurse gave me some pills and water.

The next morning, the men in the room asked me what happened last night. I told them I couldn't remember anything. The nearest neighbor to my bed was surprised and asked again about what happened last night. Honestly, I told them I couldn't remember anything at all.

Then they told me I made a lot of noise, and suddenly I jumped out of bed and began walking around. They called the nurse, who came and gave me some medicine, and I quickly slept again in my bed.

Instantly, I recognized all my pain was gone. I called the nurse and told her I wanted to walk. She told me I couldn't and wasn't allowed by the doctors. I remember we argued a lot, and she called for help, and quickly a second nurse arrived. I won the argument because I was as stubborn as they said. I jumped out of my bed; the nurses grabbed me under my arms, believing I would fall to the floor, but I didn't. I walked to the amazement of all the people in the room. The nurses were in a state of shock and called the doctors, who came and tested me. When the testing was done, they wanted me to walk all I could for three days all over the hospital, and so I did, and it was fun.

On the third day, the doctors told me that hospitals are for sick people, and even they couldn't understand what happened to me. They asked me to leave and go home because I wasn't sick anymore.

God answered our prayers, and I got my great healing miracle!

When I was a teenager, I remember my mom was very ill with an infection in her brain. Many times, coming home from school, I wanted to talk to my mother, but she was just in some kind of coma. It was very difficult for the whole family, and we worried a lot. Our doctor told us maybe, over time, Mom would get better, but he couldn't promise anything. We were afraid we would lose our mother, a terrifying thought.

A Swedish healing evangelist came to our church for a one-week revival, and one afternoon, he had a special healing and miracle service. As sick as Mom was, we carried her to the church, which was just next door to our house. Mom was sitting in the last row; she was very sick and more or less unable to follow what was going on.

The minister was preaching the Word of God, and then suddenly, he stopped and looked directly at my mother and said: "I have a word for you, madame; our Lord Jesus is healing you right now, and in a couple of days, you will be totally restored!" Then, he just continued with his preaching.

As long as I live, I will never forget my mom's healing miracle. In a couple of days, she was out of her bed, working and taking care of us all as usual.

My grandfather, Peter Kristian Falk was a good Seventh Day Adventist; he kept the sabbath, ate no pork meat, and drank no coffee. He married a Lutheran woman with the name Julia. My dad, Regner Kristian Falk, was the firstborn, and as a baby, he got baptized with a little water on his forehead in the Lutheran church.

My grandpa was struggling with heart disease, and often he spent days in his bed. The family was very poor, and when my dad turned 16 years old, he got his first professional fishing boat and fed the whole family for many years.

Brother Janson from Sweden came to my island, Bornholm, and performed revival tent meetings. The Holy Spirit was mightily moving, and people got saved, healed, and baptized in the Holy Ghost.

Rumors went all over the island, and even my grandpa heard about the miracles. First, he didn't believe in miracles, but when you are really sick and you can't take care of your family, you tend to reconsider, which he did. One day, he told my grandma to bring the preacher to his house, but as a good Seventh Day Adventist, he told him not to preach, just pray for him. As Brother Janson prayed for my grandpa, the Holy Spirit fell upon him, and he forgot everything about being a good Seventh Day Adventist

and began speaking in tongues. He got baptized in the Holy

Ghost right there, and then when brother Janson prayed for his healing.

My grandpa got the great baptism and healing miracle at the same time.

AN OLD VAUXHALL (CAR) MIRACLE.

I don't believe God is a mechanic, but I know he can fix an old car for a poor missionary.

Because we didn't have any money and not enough faith to buy a good, new car, we purchased an old English-made Vauxhall. It looked really nice, but...

The radiator was leaking water, the engine overheated all the time, and it was not good at all. After ministering to one church in Denmark, I was so frustrated about the situation and mentioned the problem in my sermon, hoping the church would give me a great offering, which they didn't. But leaving the church, a gentleman told me I could fix the problem easily by putting some raw eggs in the radiator. I did that, and it worked for a time. Every time the radiator leaked, I just put more eggs in there, but it wasn't a permanent solution to the problem.

On a trip to my home island Bornholm, together with my wife and three children, Tina, Ruben, and Gitte, the car was fully packed. On the road crossing over Sweden, reaching the ferry in Ystad to Bornholm, we made a coffee break on the roadside one very early morning. Sitting there, drinking coffee and eating the bread, suddenly I heard the sound of water hissing out of the radiator. I filled the radiator again with all the water we had and told my family to pray, hoping we could make it to the ferry. Arriving home to my parents, I asked my dad to recommend a good mechanic who could repair the radiator for as little money as possible. Many times, my dad "saved" us financially and told me to drive the old Vauxhall to his mechanic and tell him not to repair the radiator but replace it with a brand new one and send the bill to my dad's account. I was so happy and excited, and quickly, I drove the car to the mechanic's shop.

I left the car at the shop and was told to pick it up the following day. I arrived and greeted the mechanic the next morning, hoping to see a brand-new radiator in my old Vauxhall, but I was surprised to find that same old radiator. I asked why he didn't change the radiator, and he looked very strangely at me and told me there wasn't anything wrong with the old one. We entered into a discussion because I was the one with the old, broken, leaking radiator. To end our argument, the mechanic put the radiator under pressure, and to my surprise, the radiator didn't leak at all. I couldn't believe it, and I demanded more pressure on the radiator. Then the mechanic told me if he did that, the radiator would break into pieces, and I would have to pay the bill.

I got my Vauxhall miracle and never changed the radiator!

THE RED OX MIRACLE.

Full Gospel Businessmen in Esbjerg Denmark invited me to minister to mostly non-Christian businessmen at a famous restaurant called The Red Ox.

The food was delicious, and of course, the organizers served no alcohol, but how can you eat a wonderful steak without red wine? Non-Christians in Denmark will never understand why not, so they ordered themselves wine and beer.

No one got drunk, and everyone behaved properly, but here I am preaching in a not-so-comfortable environment to non-Christian businessmen.

As I was preaching, I felt the Holy Spirit telling me to give an altar call. I argued with the Spirit of God, and I thought it wasn't a good idea at all. To be honest, I was scared and afraid of the reaction.

I knew it was the Holy Spirit, and I had to do it. I told the

Holy Spirit that it was His responsibility, and if it went wrong, I just would jump in my car and leave it to the organizers.

I closed my eyes and gave the altar call, and—in my heart, I prayed all I had learned and mostly out of fear. After a while, I opened my eyes and was shocked to find everyone, yes, all of them standing in front of me, wanting prayers.

As soon as my wife Hannah and I began praying for the people, we felt the wind of the Holy Spirit blowing, and suddenly, out of nowhere, everyone was slain and nailed to the floor. People tried to get up from the floor, but it was impossible. Hannah and I left at one o'clock in the morning, and people were still on the floor. The last people left at two o'clock in the morning and the Full Gospel Businessmen had to pay an extra bill for overtime.

Did miracles really happen that night on the floor of the famous restaurant? Oh, yes!

What we didn't know when we prayed for the people was that a lady was very sick from cancer; she had been in and out of the hospital again and again. She was only skin and bones, and everyone could recognize she was in serious trouble.

The following day, she went in for another scheduled surgery. She was lying on the surgeon's table under full anesthesia, and the doctor was ready to cut her open. Suddenly, the surgeon stopped the normal procedure. He simply couldn't cut her open before he got a second x-ray. Everyone in the theater was wondering what was going on, but they had to obey the surgeon.

When the second x-ray was provided, all the cancerous tumors were simply gone, disappeared! Everyone was in shock, and the lady, when she woke up, was extremely glad and happy. What a glorious miracle. Thank you, Holy Spirit, for your guidance.

MY HOUSE MIRACLE.

In the year 1992, we had been serving God as missionaries in Tanzania since 1974. For 18 years, we had rented houses to live in, and a lot of money was paid to the owners.

One day, the Lord told me not to spend money paying rent to have a shelter to live in but process the land and build my own home.

It´s not easy to buy land in Tanzania, and the process was difficult, but with the help of the Holy Spirit, we purchased a piece of land for our ministry, New Life Outreach, and a piece to build our house.

The owners belonged to the tribe called Masai, and at that time, those people couldn't read or write. When they signed the documents, they just made a big X and added their thumb's inkprint.

When I showed the piece of property to my wife, Hannah, and asked her if she could live there if I built her a house, she smiled and said yes, but years later, she told me she meant no.

The area was a Masai village without water or electricity. All the people and especially the children, looked at us and watched us all the time every day.

It took us a little more than a year to build our house. It was very difficult for the Africans to build a home for the white man or Mzungu, as they call us. Our neighbor's homes (huts) were built with sticks and cow dung, but I wanted to build a real house for my wife and children.

The biggest problem was that I didn't have any money to build my house. We prayed a lot and believed God for everything every day.

One day, I felt the Holy Spirit lead me to a local businessman, Mr. Minde, who was very kind to us. He belonged to the Catholic Church but wasn't a follower of Jesus. Very often, I testified to him, and I knew he was very touched. I told him about my building plans, and he was very excited and told me it was the right thing to do. I told him, thank you, but I don't have any money, maybe you can help me? He was shocked and politely said sorry, then he paused, and I knew the Holy Spirit was at work. Suddenly, he said if anyone could help me, it would be Mr. Rajab, who just had opened a business selling building materials.

On the recommendation from Mr. Minde, the Catholic, I went over to Mr. Rajab, a Muslim, and boldly asked him if he could help me deliver building materials to my house. We had never met before, and he looked very strangely at me and shockingly said yes. I told him my problem—that I was a missionary without any money. Again, he looked at me with that strange look in his eyes and answered, no problem, you pay when you get money. For more than a year, Mr. Rajab provided not only building materials but also cash so I could pay my workers.

After we moved into our new home, I went to see Mr. Rajab and told him I was ready to receive my bill, and he just answered, yeah, I will prepare it for you. Again and again, I went to Mr. Rajab's shop asking for my bill, and I always got the same answer, yeah, I will prepare it for you. Finally, I got tired of asking for my bill, and I told Mr. Rajab that he had to bring it to my house if he wanted any money.

His reaction was strange; he wasn't angry but looked very confused and said, "Dr. Egon, I have a problem; I can't remember all the materials and money I gave to you."

"Mr. Rajab," I said, "you are a lucky and good man. I have recorded everything clearly and precisely in a book."

Mr. Rajab smiled and asked if he could see
the book. Of course, I gave it to him, but it still took many months before I got my bill.

I read the bill and recognized I was in a dilemma; I didn't have the money.

I decided to be open and earnest with Mr. Rajab and told him I didn't have the money. His response took me by surprise. Dr. Egon, he responded, I trust and believe in you. You have all the time you need to pay the bill—weeks, months, or even years; it doesn't matter. I know you will pay me my money.

I told Mr. Rajab I believed some Christian brothers should have helped me, but they didn't, so God chose a Muslim and that my God would surely bless you, Mr. Rajab—miraculously. He just looked at me and smiled. When I left his shop, I smiled even more.

It took me some time to pay the bill, and I apologized several times to Mr. Rajab, who told me not to worry. Then, I realized Mr. Rajab´s business began to grow bigger and bigger. Today, Mr. Rajab's business is one of the biggest in our city.

Now, when I meet Mr. Rajab, I always remind him that MY GOD is blessing him because he helped me build my house, and then he just smiles and says, yeah, I know.

Why did God bless me with a house in Arusha, Tanzania? When I sold my house in Denmark, God told me and my wife Hannah to give all the money to the mission work in Tanzania. It wasn't easy because it was a lot of money, but we obeyed and did that. That's why God blessed us with a wonderful home in Africa.

A SPEAKING IN TONGUES MIRACLE.

As our mission work in Tanzania was growing and increasing, we needed to buy a trailer to hold our equipment when we had our outreaches, and therefore, we went to a known factory in Denmark.

The day we bought the trailer, the factory owner told his family at suppertime about the meeting with us. Immediately, the owner's son said he wanted to go to Tanzania and stay with the missionaries. Since the family belonged to the Danish Lutheran Church, the dad didn't like his son's idea.

After arguing for some time, the family decided to meet with us, which we agreed to. After talking for a while, I asked the son from this family if he was saved, a born-again Christian, and his response was, YES! Finally, the family allowed the son to come and stay with us in Tanzania.

One time, we went on an outreach to the Barabaig tribe, who didn't know anything about Jesus. This tribe was dangerous, and many people were killed because young men were not allowed to get married before they could prove they were real men by killing another human from another tribe with only a spear. It was also acceptable to kill an elephant or a lion, but a human was the absolute best.

In the years 1975 and 1976, I tried to reach this tribe but failed. By making friends and reaching out to those people, I wanted to give them the Gospel of Jesus Christ, but they became very angry and hostile with me.

Now, about 20 years later, and together with this young man from Denmark, we went to the Barabaig tribe again. Tanzania's government had built a primary school for the children, and the head teacher allowed me to preach to the kids, and later, we were supposed to hold an open-air meeting.

As I was preaching, the young man from Denmark was outside the school building, and suddenly, he experienced something which terrified him.

My preaching was interrupted because two neighboring tribes were tired of getting killed by the Barabaig tribe all the time. They had decided to finish them off, yes, all of them to bring peace.

It was very dangerous and chaotic, and we had to leave the area quickly.

We traveled to Singida, where my family and I lived in 1974 when we arrived in Tanzania for the first time. I asked the Pentecostal Church pastor if I could have a church meeting, and even though it wasn't planned or announced, it didn't take long before the church was packed with people.

The Holy Spirit began to move powerfully, and people got baptized in the Holy Ghost and spoke in tongues.

The young man from Denmark suddenly came to me at the

platform. He was close to being in shock, and his face was totally white; he almost screamed in my ears and pointed to a lady, saying he could clearly hear her speak in the Danish language.

Since I knew the lady, I also knew she was not speaking Danish.

I mean, she was NOT able to speak in our Danish language, not a single word. She only knew how to speak her mother tongues, Kinyatulu and Kiswahili.

I told this young man from Denmark that if this lady spoke Danish, he better go and listen carefully. He went down to her to listen, and YES, she spoke by the Holy Spirit without ever knowing she was speaking the Danish language only because of this young man from Denmark.

After the service, when we left the church, this young guy reminded me about questioning him whether he was saved and born again the first time we met in Denmark. He said, "I answered you honestly out of my understanding as a Lutheran that I was saved and born again." Then, he looked at me and added, but now I really know I am saved and born again, and Jesus is the Lord of my life.

A SICK DEMON UNDERSTANDS SWAHILI IN DENMARK MIRACLE.

One Sunday morning, I was ministering in a church in Denmark, and my text was from Matthew 17:14-18 about Jesus healing a boy with a demon. The boy's dad told Jesus, "He has seizures and is suffering greatly. He often falls into the fire or into water."

I carefully explained to the congregation that there is a physical illness called epilepsy, where demons are not involved. Then you have the kind of demonic epilepsy manifesting through seizures as the boy in the text.

The physical illness called epilepsy is treated by doctors medically, and believers of Jesus prayerfully bring healing as the Bible teaches us. It is not healing the sick by casting out demons when it's not demonic. But the kind of epilepsy the boy had was demonic, and that's why Jesus rebuked the demon, and it came out of the boy, and he was healed from that moment.

After the service, a young lady confronted me. She was very angry and shouted loudly, "So, I am demon possessed because I have epilepsy?" I really tried to calm her down and told her I would never tell her she was possessed by demons. I tried to explain the text once more; it helped, but she left me angry. By the way, she didn't want me to pray for her either.

After a couple of weeks, I ministered in a tent meeting, and when I gave the altar call, many people responded. As I was praying for people, suddenly I heard a lady scream very loudly, and I knew it was demons. I followed the noise and found my wife, Hannah, praying for the same lady who had angrily confronted me on Sunday morning in church a couple of weeks ago.

When my wife recognized the lady, she instantly knew it was the demonic kind of epilepsy and not the physical. When she rebuked the demon, she did this not in the Danish language but in Kiswahili in order for the angry lady not to be upset again. Instantly, when my wife rebuked the demon in the Kiswahili language, the demon understood and left the lady by screaming wildly. At that moment, the lady was completely healed.

A LUTHERAN MONEY MIRACLE.

A friend and former Danish missionary to Tanzania, Ove Petersen, planted a church in Løgstør and invited us to come for a meeting. He told us he only had 15 people, and all of them were from the bottom of the society but new, born-again Christians. Ove let us know not to expect too much; his people were new to Christianity and the Word and were also very poor. I told my friend I could minister to them free of charge, but he said no, they had some money, and also, he would take up an offering for our mission work in Tanzania.

After we ministered and prayed for all 15 or so people,

Hannah and I talked with a couple who asked a lot of questions about our work in Tanzania, especially about our New Life Schools.

Before they said goodnight and left us, they bought some of my books and asked if we needed some money. No people in Denmark had asked us so directly if we needed money, and we were taken by surprise, but we told them in detail that we needed a lot of money for our mission works.

Yes, I expected and was ready to get some money. Yes, I felt it was God, but finally, the gentleman said okay and goodnight! I was stunned when I saw them walk out of the building. Was it a joke? If so, it was a bad joke, mocking us and our mission work.

After some days, this gentleman called our New Life Outreach office, investigating if we were real and if our office would send him a written letter to confirm the truth of our ministry. He then would transfer USD 50,000 toward our building project for one of our schools in Tanzania.

Later, I called this gentleman to thank him for his generosity and found out one of my books had greatly impacted him. This gentleman and his family belonged to the Lutheran Church of Denmark, and it was a big money miracle for him and us as well.

A STORMY WINDY MIRACLE BLOWING WITH A GREAT POWER.

I grew up next to the ocean, and on stormy days, water from the big waves hit my house's windows.

For me to have the freedom to walk anywhere I wanted, my dad demanded that I learn to swim in the big ocean. I was very proud when I proved to my dad that I could conquer the big water, and he approved my freedom.

Now, I could go all over the place, and nothing could stop me. I felt like a king and ruler.

One day, I went to the top of a cliff, proudly showing off my strength for my best friend by lifting a big rock over my head and throwing it into the ocean. After showing off several times, I lost my footing, and in a split-second, I knew I was on my way to die. It was a terrifying moment, which I still can feel. Then, out of nowhere, a mighty wind took me back to the cliff. I wasn't able to see the wind, but I could hear it and certainly felt it. I was in shock, and my whole body was shivering, knowing an angel from Heaven just saved me. YES, I STILL BELIEVE IN ANGELS!

A JUMPING CAR MIRACLE IN NORWAY.

From 1970 to 1974, we lived in Norway, where I was on the road almost every week, having revival meetings everywhere. Hannah, my wife, had to stay at home because of our two small children.

After being away from my family for an extended period, I was rushing home. I was homesick like crazy, and I wanted to see my family.

Coming close to my village, I was driving downhill on a very narrow road. The road was cut out of the mountain, and on the other side was a big, deep lake.

It was winter with a lot of snow and ice. I was used to the road and knew every pothole and corner. I know I was driving fast, but I kept to my side. Suddenly, in a very sharp bend, a big truck driving uphill cut the corner and was right in front of me. I instantly knew we would have a frontal collision, and I didn't have any chance to survive.

I can still hear myself screaming with all the power of my lungs the name of Jesus, and then I passed over the big truck. My heart was pounding as I tried to catch my breath. I recognized that Jesus had given me a not-so-normal miracle and saved my life from a horrible death.

Shortly after, my neighbor was driving downhill, following my car tracks, and then he surprisingly recognized that the tracks stopped and appeared again further down the road.

THE FOOD MIRACLE.

When we lived in Norway, we were very poor, but somehow, we never worried about anything; we simply trusted God, who called us to His ministry.

I remember one evening eating absolutely the last food we had in our house. We had no money to buy any more food.

Trusting God, we went to bed and slept all night peacefully. The next morning, I wanted to leave the house, but something outside the door blocked it, and I had to use all my shoulder power to force open the door. When outside, I was surprised to see a lot of big boxes blocking the door. Every box was loaded with groceries that would last for a long time. I tell you—we had a feast!

I wanted to know who gave us all the groceries but failed to figure it out.

During the 50 years of full-time ministry, God, our Heavenly Father, has often sent "ravens" to our house.

THE JAR MIRACLE.

I was on the road for eight weeks, preaching in revival meetings. I didn't go home and have a break with my family because I didn't have the travel money to do it.

Often, I left my wife Hannah without any or very little money, and she had to trust God for the daily bread. Hannah never had money to buy bread and to save just a little money, she baked bread herself to feed her and our two small children.

Hannah had a special jar for flour, and when I came home after being on the road for eight weeks, she went to the kitchen to bake me some bread. After a while, she came crying into our small living room, and I asked what was wrong. Her answer blew me away. She told me that she had only bought flour one time during the eight weeks, and she baked bread using the flour from the jar, and it was always full to the brim. It was impossible to empty the jar!

Would I ever again leave my wife and children behind without any provision????

MY WIFE´S THYROID HEALING MIRACLE.

In the 90s, my wife Hannah fell ill. She is not a woman who goes to a doctor before it's needed. She is a tough lady who believes in God. She is not against doctors, but she believes more in God our Father than any doctor. Hannah won't lay down until she is not able to stand on her feet. Hannah was sick a long time before I recognized anything. The first thing we did was gear up our faith, praying and believing God for her healing, but she got worse.

We went to see a local doctor in Arusha where we were living, who we trusted, but the situation was too difficult for him, and he sent us to a specialist at Nairobi Hospital in Kenya. The specialist was a nice doctor from the U.S., and after all the tests, he found the source of the illness. On the spot, he told us three options: number one radiation, number two surgery, and number three medication. Before Hannah could answer what she wanted, he said, "Let's first try medication." Hannah and I went back home to Arusha, Tanzania, with medication for three months. We still prayed and believed God for healing, and after three months on the medication, we went back to see the American specialist at the Nairobi Hospital in Kenya. He was very optimistic and believed the medication would cure Hannah completely and gave her more medication for the next three months.

After a couple of months, Hannah got really ill, and I had to take her back to the specialist, who was very surprised about her situation. Quickly, he ran several tests on my wife, and when he gave us the results, we could have jumped for joy. He said the medication had become poison to her body because she was already totally healed! A healthy person doesn't need any medication. Go home and don't touch the medication, and within a couple of weeks, you will be totally fine, he said.

We traveled back home, threw away all the medication, and through today, Hannah has been healed and will continue to be well.

FOUR TALL ANGELS.

I had to travel to the Muslim island of Zanzibar for a crusade and seminar. I left my wife Hannah alone at our home in Olosiva, Arusha.

At that time, our area wasn't safe, and several people were murdered just next to our house. I was concerned for my wife's safety, but Hannah was confident and felt safe and told me to go ahead and travel.

Later, Hannah told me she felt safe and peaceful because she saw four very tall angels protecting our home, one at each corner of our property.

We had bought our land from a Masai family with the name Mollel. At that time, they couldn't read or write, and when they signed the documents, they made an X and an ink fingerprint.

INTO AFRICA

Egon enjoys being among Africans.

Chapter Nine
THE DANISH AFRICAN
By Pastor Geir Stomnås

Most people are meant to remain in their native ambiance, building their homes, going to work, and staying close to their relatives.

But some people receive such a strong divine calling upon their lives that they are willing to leave their home country and settle in a distant world. Among the last group are Egon and Hannah. They have my deepest respect. When they first left their families and friends in the seventies to work as missionaries in Tanzania, no one except God was able to know that it was the first step in a lifetime of ministry.

Geir Stomnås is pastor in the pentecostal church Filadelfia Vennesla in Norway

My wife and I have been a small part of their lives and ministry since 2006. The first years we had the pleasure of receiving them in the Filadelfia-Church in Vennesla, Norway.

Since 2011, we have had the privilege of participating in the crusades in Tanzania. I have also given lectures at the Bible college in Arusha. Our relationship with Egon and Hannah is not just professional, but we have developed a friendship during the years. Their lovely home is always open for us when we stay in Tanzania. The nights in Arusha and the long trips to the crusades have led to many good conversations.

All who come close to them will feel the strong need in their hearts to bring the lost and beloved people into God´s kingdom. I am impressed that they are still on fire after all these years. Nothing gives greater joy to their hearts than seeing people being saved. A few years ago, we were sitting together in the living room in their home, the evening before we should leave for the crusade. Then Hannah said, "I am starting to get excited. During the next days, we will again see hundreds of people being delivered and coming to Christ. All the problems we are facing are worth fighting for when I think about these souls. This is what we live for."

I can't write about Egon without mentioning Hannah. The two of them are more than a couple. They are truly one in the Lord's ministry. Therefore, it is unnatural to say "Egon" and not "Egon and Hannah." These two names have become a common expression when we mention the work we are supporting in Tanzania.

Egon is in the front. He is the preacher of the gospel among thousands of people in the African bush. His loud voice is heard when the demons are driven out in the name of Jesus. He is the one who runs with the healed cripples on stage and who appears in most of the photos and films. But Egon without Hannah is like a body without arms and legs. It is like a car without tires. Prov 31: 10-31 is about a wife of noble character. She is worth far more than rubies. Her husband has full confidence in her and lacks nothing of value. This is a description of Hannah. I have seen them working together and how she supports and takes care of her husband in all situations. In Norway, we have a saying, "Behind every successful man, there is a strong woman." It couldn't be more true than in the case of Egon and Hannah. The anointing steams out of the two of them through their powerful unity in the Lord Jesus Christ.

Egon in action is a special sight. It is like he is having supernatural contact with the participants present at the crusades. In one moment, the people laugh when he makes some funny illustrations with his body and voice. The next moment, there might be a deep silence when the people are filled with awe in front of the Almighty God. When he invites the people to receive Jesus at the end of his sermon, a huge crowd rushes to the front. When the worship team starts to play and sing together with his prayers and the people are stretching out their hands toward Heaven, it is a holy moment. Tears stream down the faces of those experiencing God's love and grace. It is like an explosion when Egon, in the name of Jesus, commands the evil spirits and sicknesses to leave the wrecked bodies and souls. Everyone can hear the screams of the demons when they are cast out. They can see with their own eyes how people that couldn't walk before now are running at the stage. Egon is the fastest man in the world at a distance of 30 yards. When the Spirit is upon him, and he rejoices because of the Lord's mighty work, no one can follow him. I am a runner myself, and in all other distances, I would have crushed him. But on the 30 yards at the stage, I have no chance.

The most honorable words a missionary can receive is when the natives say, "You have become like one of us." Egon was born a Dane, and he will always have his Danish citizenship. But his language and heart are African. If it weren't for his bright skin, no one could separate him from the Tanzanian. Both his inner thoughts and mind and his outward behavior express his true being. He has turned into a Dane-African, or maybe it is more correct to say an African Dane.

I have always admired Egon for his huge faith. He knows that our mighty God will respond when he calls upon the name of Jesus. He has seen the power of the Spirit released again and again. This has increased his expectations. And the end has not yet come. I am sure that the next decade will be as powerful as the formers. I pray that God will give both him and Hannah good health so that this couple of fire may continue to spread the gospel as long as they breathe.

Chapter Ten
THE MASAI TRIBE

Who doesn't know the typical picture of a Masai, dressed in red, looking out toward the never-ending savanna? For years and years, this African tribe has received respect and a lot of attention because they have managed to protect their traditional way of life, which in several ways can be occultic.

The Masai tribe was first mentioned about 200 years B.C. as the shepherd people who honored their cattle and traveled far with them to find green grass. In the 18th century, this tribe dominated big areas of East Africa.

The Masai tribe still believes they are the chosen tribe of God and have ownership of all cattle on the earth. They have often enforced this "right" and stolen all the cattle they wanted from other tribes. The Masais are not known to give in to other tribes, and they are known to be warriors. During the time of the slave trade, the slave traders stayed out of their way.

The cow is a holy animal to the Masai, and the cow gives them everything they need. Milk is an essential part of their daily food. The milk is mixed with blood from the cattle or fermented with cow urine and grass ash. Meat is only for special occasions.

Many Masais don't know fear; they are self-sufficient and

proud of nature, and that's why their culture has survived big changes. Even though they are only two percent of Tanzania's inhabitants, which has 130 different tribes, the Masai, together with the lion, are well-known African symbols.

The Masais have never been hunters, but they will protect their cattle fiercely and will kill a lion if they have to.

Traditionally, it's the younger children, mostly girls and women, who dominate the Masai village. The men are out herding the cattle and will return home in the evening.

It's the women who do the most and hardest jobs in their Boma (village). They look after the kids, of which there are many; they milk the cows, cook, and build their huts cleaned up from cow dung.

Masai can literally leap high for joy. Here, a Masai leaps in excitement on stage at one of Egon Falk's miracle campaigns.

The Masai dance consists of a deep roar, almost measuring while they one by one jump high into the air with a loud scream like they had springs under their feet. These jumps are a sign of their strength and manhood.

Today, many Masai are giving their lives to Jesus, and they are the most devoted and faithful followers. One of our former coworkers, a Masai, was beaten repeatedly by his father because he got saved. He was bigger and stronger than his father and could easily have avoided the beating, but he showed his father respect and endured the suffering until his father gave up.

Through the years, we have supported several Masai evangelists and also trained them in our Bible school. Today, we have several co-workers from the Masai tribe, and they are a blessing to us.

Esaya, one of the Masai evangelists we supported, planted a church among his own tribe, and we did a revival meeting with him in a Government Primary School.

In one of the services, a Masai warrior came to the front and wanted to receive Jesus and be saved. I asked him to kneel, and I would pray for him. His answer surprised me; he was really stubborn and loudly shouted NO. Since he interrupted my preaching and by his own will came down to the front and wanted to receive Jesus, I was confused. I asked him again if he wanted me to pray for him, and the response was loud and clear, YES!

Again, I told him to kneel so I could pray for him, and again, he shouted NO, which was repeated several times.

Finally, I had to ask him why he didn't want to kneel, and his answer was mind-blowing to the white mzungu missionary—me. He whispered in my ear, "Too many women are looking at me." A Masai worrier can't publicly kneel when women are present; it's just too humbling in their culture.

I guided him into a side room without any women looking at us and told him to kneel, and can you believe it? Again, his response was loud and clear NO. I looked at him and asked him, "Where are all the women?"

He said there were none! The Masai warrior

looked deep into my eyes and proudly told me no man could meet God with a weapon in his belt. He then loosened his belt, and together with his big Masai knife, put it down on the floor. Then, with a big smile on his face, he knelt and told me to pray for him.

Do you think this Masai warrior got saved? Oh, yes, he was born again and received the greatest miracle ever!

THE MASAI WORRIER AND THE BLOOD.

The Masai people love to drink blood directly from the animal's neck vein and mix the blood with milk. When they slaughter a cow, for example, they kill it by strangulation so all the blood will go to the stomach, and then they open up the stomach and kneel, putting their heads down to the stomach and licking the blood, just like dogs. Often, it seems as if they are going into a trance.

A pastor friend of mine, a Masai warrior, once told me about their culture and traditions, which are very interesting, and when he came to the blood, he somehow was taken away, and his face lit up in happiness. Looking at me, he added, now, I am saved. I have a new culture, and I don't drink blood anymore.

THE MASAI WARRIOR AND THE HOLY SPIRIT.

During a crusade and seminar for the Masai tribe, I taught about the Holy Spirit, and coming to the last day, we prayed for them all to be baptized in the Holy Ghost.

Masai warriors can´t show any feelings publicly; it´s a sign of weakness. If they cry, you really have humiliated and conquered them.

As we were praying, suddenly the Holy Spirit fell upon all the Masai warriors, who cried loudly with tears streaming down their faces, and yes, they prayed in the Heavenly language, tongues.

At the end of the service, a Masai warrior came to me and asked for my permission to speak. He asked his wife to join him, and he put his arm around her neck and shoulder, which is against their culture because it's a sign of weakness for the man. He then said, "I have beaten you so many times; now, I know it's wrong, and I promise you in front of everyone I will never beat you again!"

THE MASAI WARRIOR AND WORSHIP.

When I bought the land for our house from the Mollel family, there was a small piece, a corner, they didn't want to sell me—maybe later, they told me. I couldn't understand why, but a few years later, I figured it out.

After we moved into our home (boma), the leaders or elders of the Mollel family told me to follow their Masai tradition and make them a feast in my boma. I agreed to their request, and we threw them a feast, telling them no alcohol (pombe) would be served because we are followers of Christ Jesus. The Masai warriors love pombe and meat, and many of them are alcoholics. Often, they get drunk, and children are born without knowing who their fathers are because their mothers can't remember anything at all.

During this feast, the Mollel leaders blessed me, and I became one of their leaders when they legally gave me their family name Mollel, which I still carry today.

After some time, the Mollel elders came to me and offered to sell me this corner of land if I promised not to touch the one tree on the land. We agreed, and I got the land, respecting not to touch the tree.

On our new land, there was a lot of demonic activity going on, especially at nighttime. Many of our visitors couldn't sleep at all, and our Masai guards were often terrified.

I figured out there was something about this tree I promised not to touch. We began to pray about that tree, and the more we prayed, the stronger the demonic activity was, but after a while, I recognized the tree was dying, and one day, it just couldn't live anymore and fell over. Now, I touched the tree and made it into firewood!

When the elders and leaders of the Mollel family saw their

"sacred" tree dead, they were stunned by the white man's (mzungu) God.

Under that tree, the Masai people worshipped the god of Mount Meru and entered into occult demonic worship.

Now, this corner of land is a part of our Academy of Leadership Bible school, where we worship our Almighty and Living God!

A SOCCER BALL MIRACLE.

One Sunday afternoon, after our New Life City Church service, Hannah and I were sitting outside in our garden, having a cup of coffee and just enjoying our own fellowship. Outside the hedge, a group of young boys played soccer on an open field.

I asked my wife if she had a leather soccer ball. Hannah didn't have any interest in the soccer game, so why I asked her, I don't know. Her answer, of course, was no, but then she paused and said, just wait a minute, and I will have a look in the house. Believe it or not, after a few minutes, she came out with a big smile on her face with a real leather soccer ball and a pump.

With joy in my heart, I called to the boys who were playing with a homemade soccer ball made from plastic, paper, and pieces of fabric. I told them I loved them and wanted to bless them with a brand-new real leather soccer ball. Their eyes got big with excitement and thankfulness, which I will never forget. Just an ordinary leather soccer ball created joy and happiness for the poor African boys. That night, I slept with a smile on my face, thinking about those boys' futures.

Only a couple of days later, somebody slipped a letter through the gate to my house. It was addressed to me, and 31 young boys thanked and blessed me for the real leather soccer ball I gave to them that Sunday afternoon. The boys also had a question, would I be their Father? As I was reading, my heart was pounding; I was touched, and I had to ask myself what I could possibly do for 31 young African boys.

My answer was a BIG yes, and today, many years later, we have the New Life Soccer Club, which impacts many young boys.

Three years ago, when I was teaching a new class at our Academy of Leadership Bible school, I looked repeatedly at a young man. There was something about him, and I had to ask who he was. It turned out that he was the young boy who wrote the letter, asking me to be the 31 young soccer boys' father. Frank Mollel is his name, and he belongs to the Mollel family, who sold me the land to build my house and the Bible school. Today, Frank is a minister of the Gospel of Jesus Christ and serves God with all his heart.

Through a soccer ball, many young boys now know Jesus and have a bright future!

THE LAIZER CLAN.

As an elder and leader of the Mollel family, I attended the leaders' meetings many times, and I learned to be strong. Only by being strong could I win respect from the rival family clan called Laizer.

When I built my house (boma), we didn't have any water, and nobody can exist without water. I had a tractor and trailer with a big tank that went around buying water to bring to our house every week.

Finally, I got permission from the Secretary of Defense to connect a water line to a government official's house, which had water from a military line. It was far from my house, and I spent a lot of money on the waterline, but we got water. Our joy of having water in our home was short-lived. Since I now was a Mollel, I became an enemy to the Laizer clan, and they sabotaged my waterline again and again.

The Mollel elders told me, if I didn't show my power as a Mollel warrior, the Laizer clan would come and burn down my house. I asked the elders what to do, and they told me to arrest the leader from the Laizer clan. With the help of a police officer, the top leader was arrested and put behind bars.

The next morning, a young warrior from the Laizer clan came to my house, and as soon I appeared, he was on his knees begging for forgiveness. He said I could punish him for their top leader's wrongdoing, and if I wanted, I could even kill him. I told him I wanted to kill him but couldn't because I was a Christian and a follower of Christ. I told him my forgiveness would be released when their top leader had signed a written document, promising never to harm my waterline again and even to protect it.

The document was approved by the judge, who called for the top leader from the Laizer clan. When the police brought him into the courtroom, the judge read the document and asked if he would agree and sign it, but the Laizer top leader was stubborn and shouted a big NO! The judge ordered the police to take the Laizer clan leader back behind bars at the prison.

The judge told me not to worry anymore, and he promised that no one from the Laizer clan would ever touch my waterline.

Hannah Falk is seen in the background with the Christian Masai women.

After some time, the top leader from the Laizer clan was released from prison, and I haven't seen him since. I have asked about him several times, and I'm told he is around, but he hides every time he sees me. Now, we have peace between the Mollel and Laizer clans.

As I was working with the elders of my "clan," I recognized that they weren't interested in any kind of development for their families and society. The only interest the elders had was getting money out of me and getting drunk.

When the Mollel elders adopted me, they showed me the importance of being a strong leader. So, one day at our meeting, I told them off—all of them. I was adamant and blunt with them and a little scared as well, but I recognized I had them in my hand. I told them I was wasting my time and money, and from now on, they were not welcome to my boma (house). I told them they were bad leaders—being drunk husbands and fathers, and as I was leaving the meeting, I told them I wasn't coming back. From now on, I would take their families and give them Jesus together with education. They were shocked and in a state of disbelief when I left the room with a loud Goodbye!

With the help of my son, Ruben, and his wife, Hanne, we took the first steps, which today is New Life Schools with almost 900 children and youngsters.

Chapter Eleven
EXTRAORDINARY AND POWERFUL MIRACLES

I always have many demons manifesting at my crusades, and sometimes it is very wild and violent. If you don't know what's going on, it can be very frightening as well.

THE PUNCH.

A gentleman possessed by demons came forward every day for help and prayers, and every day, some demons left him.

Finally, he was in the line of people who wanted to testify about their salvation, healing, and deliverance, and this gentleman was in the line as well. As he came close to me, suddenly all the demons attacked him, and he became very violent. I was totally taken by surprise, and, not being myself, I punched him with all my power directly in his stomach, and he dropped like a dead man. Now, I was terrified; I looked at him and realized he was still breathing. All the pastors came and wanted to help, but I told them to leave him alone on the floor while I continued to minister to the people.

After a long time, this gentleman came to his consciousness and was on his feet. I was afraid he would remember that I hit him in the stomach, but thank God, he couldn't remember anything and just wondered why he was on the floor. After testing him, I knew that he was completely free of any satanic demons, and what a joy it was.

THE WATER.

Sometimes, the demons leave instantly, and other times, the deliverance goes on for several days.

A petite lady without a lot of physical muscle power became very strong during the deliverance; it was like a war every day. At last, she testified that she was free and saved by the grace of God.

Sunday night, we did the water baptismal on my stage, and hundreds of people lined up, and so did this little lady. Again, she testified and proclaimed Jesus as her Lord and Savior, but instantly, when her feet touched the water, all hell broke loose. I needed four to six strong gentlemen to hold and control her. The pastors looked at me and asked what to do. My answer shocked them. I told them to get her under the water, but they were not willing to do so. I told them the devil is afraid of water and just wanted to stop this lady from doing the right thing. In the name of the Father, the Son, and the Holy Ghost, she came under the water and was baptized, and when she came out of the water, she was totally delivered and free.

THE BIG COOKING POT.

I did a big and powerful crusade in Dar Es Salaam, the biggest city of Tanzania. Thousands of people attended every day.

One afternoon, some people, who I never found out who they were (angels?) went into a room at Muhimbili, the biggest hospital in Tanzania, and picked up a very sick Muslim gentleman who also was a witch doctor from Sumbawanga, a city in the Southern part of the country.

This Muslim witch doctor came to Dar Es Salaam to "treat" people with his satanic powers. For months, he "ministered" to the people right where my stage was built, but then he got sick and was hospitalized. Now, he was only skin and bones, not able to walk a single step.

As he was lying in the grass, listening to my preaching when I prayed for people, something powerful hit him, and he was saved and healed. He stood on his feet and came to the stage to tell the multitudes about the power of Jesus. All of us were rejoicing and worshipping God for His mercy and grace.

Suddenly, this Muslim witch doctor looked at me, saying his wife got saved the day before. We called her to the stage, and when she came, this Muslim witch doctor somehow became uncomfortable and said, "Dr. Egon, something is wrong. She is not my wife."

"Why?" I asked. Then he told all of us that they just lived together but were not legally married. Wow! Some Christians just live together without being married, and if you touch the subject, they react angrily, but the Muslim witch doctor, under the power of the Holy Spirit, instantly knew it wasn't right.

He looked at me and said, "Dr. Egon, can you make it right with God and marry us?"

I replied, of course, I will and can, but it has to be organized. Now, he shouted, "No, No, No, I can't leave your stage without being right with God. Marry us NOW, Dr. Egon." And so I did in front of at least 30,000 guests.

Then, I told them to leave my stage, but again the Muslim witch doctor looked at me with a big smile and said, we need to be baptized in water first, then we will leave. Again, I was surprised. Christians argue about water baptism, but now the Muslim witch doctor was demanding to be baptized here and now, and he wanted enough water to get totally under and immersed in it.

We could not organize it then and there, but I told them to come to our Sunday morning service in a rented auditorium.

Sunday morning, I walked into the big auditorium, which had a Hindu temple at the rear end and my stage opposite. I looked at my stage and saw a big cooking pot, black from smoke, used to cook red beans and rice for big celebrations but now full of water for another and greater celebration.

In my fantasy, I saw the white missionary walking into a small African village, preaching the Gospel, ending up in the witch doctor's cooking pot. However, today, the witch doctor himself, by his own free will, ended up in the cooking pot, being baptized in the name of the Father, the Son Jesus, and the Holy Spirit. With the help of my good friend, Pastor Frank Bailey from New Orleans, Louisiana, we got the witch doctor under the water, which spilled all over. The next person in the cooking pot was the witch doctor's wife; oh, what a glorious moment! I got so excited, looked at the congregation, lifted my hand, and shouted, "What is to hinder you? Here is water!"

Instantly, people lined up for the baptism, and the next person, a tall young man, was already in the cooking pot. I asked him, "Have you received Jesus as Savior and Lord?"

"NO," he answered.

To my own surprise, I asked him, "What are you doing in the cooking pot then?"

He looked at me with a unique light in his eyes and answered, "I want to be saved, born again, and baptized in water."

Pastor Frank Bailey and I got him under the water, and he became a newborn young man changed by the power of the Gospel of Jesus Christ.

As we continued baptizing people, one of the local pastors whispered in my ear, "Dr. Egon, what you are doing here is wrong."

I was shocked and angered by him and asked him what we were doing wrong, and his answer irritated me even more. He said, "People need to be baptized in the white baptismal robes."

Now, I really got upset, but thank God for the Holy Spirit. I looked at him and told him about the 3,000 people in Jerusalem who, on the day of Pentecost, got saved and baptized in water all on the same day. Oh, yes, this pastor knew that story and liked it. I asked him if he believed the same thing could happen in his city. Yes, he believed that and wanted it to happen. I looked deep in his eyes and told him to go and buy at least 3,000 white baptismal robes—and by the way, pay for it yourself. Now, he was shivering and looked at me, saying he didn't have that kind of money, so Dr. Egon go ahead with the baptism, and so I did. Water was splashing all over, and my people had to bring many more buckets of water to the cooking pot.

About six or seven months later, I met the witch doctor again. He was happily telling me that he was now baptized in the Holy Ghost. "Dr. Egon," he said, "I want to serve Jesus as you do!"

THE FLYING MASAI.

I did a crusade at the border to Kenya called Namanga, and on the day of arrival, the expectation was big. Without any problems,
the authorities allowed us to cross the border, announcing the crusade for the Kenyans and Tanzanians at the same time.

Sitting on my stage, listening to the welcome speeches and church choirs singing, suddenly I saw a Masai warrior with a big machete in his hand, jumping and "flying" from the ground over the front of my stage and crash-landing right in front of me and

my wife. He was lying there like a dead person. Everyone was in shock and didn't do anything. I jumped up, pushing away the big machete, and began praying for him, knowing in my spirit he was possessed by demons. My people took over and ministered to him until he was set free from all the demons. Yes, he got saved, born again, and changed by the power of the Gospel.

Later, he told us that before his grandfather died, he had asked him to take his big machete to kill the white (mzungu) missionary evangelist who would come and preach the Gospel of Jesus Christ in order for his spirit to come and watch over his burial site.

Thank God that the ONE who lives in me is greater than the one who lives in the world.

GUEST ROOM NUMBER FIVE.

I have realized that the greatest miracles happen when you preach the Gospel, as Jesus said in Mark 16:17-18. "These signs will accompany those who believe: In my name, they will drive out demons; they will speak in new tongues, they will pick up snakes with their hands; and when they drink deadly poison, it will not hurt them at all; they will place their hands on sick people, and they will get well."

As I was preaching for 10-15,000 people, words suddenly came out of my mouth, and I wondered where they came from. I shouted very loudly, and my P.A. system carried the messages into the center of the city. "Listen, you gentleman, you who are in bed with a prostitute in room number five at the hotel. You are hiding it from your wife, but you can't hide from God who sees you right now!" Everyone looked at me, it was strange, but I had to ignore it and continue my preaching.

At the hotel, in room number five, was a businessman in bed with a prostitute, and he got terrified and quickly stopped his business and repented his sin. He was a backslidden believer and brought his wife and children to my crusade, telling them he quickly had to go to town for some business and would come and join his family later.

Many times, he asked me over and over how I knew it was guest room number five at the hotel. I didn't know, and there was no way I possibly would know, but God knows and God only.

DEMONIC RAINSTORMS.

Open-air crusades and rain don't go hand in hand. One time, a mighty rainstorm destroyed a lot of my crusade equipment. The wind came with great force and turned and twisted everything into pieces. Water and mud were all over my P.A. system.

As I was preaching, I saw the heavy dark clouds coming toward the crusade ground, and suddenly, the storm changed direction and disappeared behind us. Thanking God in my heart, I continued my preaching without knowing the powerful storm behind us had suddenly changed direction. It now came like thousands of demons directly to the crusade ground.

I shouted with all my power to the thousands of people, "Run, run, run, and save yourself from this demonic storm." People took off
running, and others tried to save some of my equipment, but it was impossible.

In a few minutes, there was a flood of water all over; roads were destroyed and houses as well.

My wife Hannah and I hid in our Toyota Land Cruiser, and after an hour or so, suddenly, everything became calm and silent.

I was totally devastated and somehow in a state of shock. I remember I didn't speak for 24 hours. After a couple of days, I got an email from Reinhard Bonnke, which took me out of the darkness and depression.

I remember I told the devil that he would regret and pay for all the damages, and I would not cancel any planned crusades. God showed up, and all my equipment was replaced and restored; we didn't cancel any crusades.

In the village of Handeni, which has a great number of Muslims, I did a crusade on a soccer field. I never do crusades in the rainy season, and this was the dry season with a blue sky and sunshine. However, one day, big, heavy, dark clouds with a lot of water came closer and closer to the soccer field. All the Christians prayed boldly and without shame and demanded that the clouds stop. I recognized some of the Muslims were mocking and laughing at us, but the Spirit of God came over me, and I demanded that the rain not come any closer, and it stopped right at the four borders of the soccer field. All the time I was preaching and ministering to the people, the heavy rain was pouring down just outside the soccer field, and I tell you, it didn't touch the field at all. The rain came down with force so strong, and nobody could leave until after we finished the service.

Still, some Muslims continued mocking us and said it wasn't God at all, and it made me "angry" in my spirit, not angry at the people, but angry at the devil. The next evening, I prophesied that no more rain would interrupt our crusade, but the mocking continued, so I told the whole village that rain would come back and hit them Monday afternoon when my team and equipment were leaving. When I recognized what I had just said, I got very concerned, and I also asked God for forgiveness if I had taken it too far.

Monday afternoon, when we all left the village, suddenly it began to rain heavily. God proved himself to be a faithful God, and I bowed down and worshipped Him with a humble heart.

Many weeks later, a gentleman came to my house in Arusha, which is very far from the village of Handeni. He greeted me with great honor and told me he came from Handeni and was sent by the local government to ask me to pray to my God to stop the rain. He said, "It's more than enough!"

I just can't stop loving my God!!!

EGON IN SANYA JUU.

Sanya Juu is a small village just at the foot of the majestic Kilimanjaro mountain.

It was the last day of a successful crusade when I prayed for hundreds of people who filled the open space in front of my stage.

I have many people helping me, praying for the many people and the many needs, and usually, I just lead in mass prayers without laying hands on people. There are simply too many.

I was at the front edge of my stage, praying over the masses, and suddenly, a lady grabbed my trousers. My first and quick reaction was to get rid of her, but she was very strong, and the only way out of the situation was to loosen my belt and let the trousers go, but I couldn't do that in front of 15,000 people. I didn't know anything about this lady and why she had grabbed ahold of my trousers. Desperately, she held on to my pants as I decided to ignore her and continued to pray for the masses. Suddenly, she let go of me, and I jumped away from her.

Since it was the last night of the crusade and we left early the next morning, I forgot all about this lady. Two years later, I returned to Sanya Juu and had another crusade, and on the first day, a smiling lady was allowed to enter my stage, and she had an amazing testimony.

"Two years ago," she said, "I was very sick and couldn't have any children. My loving husband took me to many of the best hospitals and doctors, but all of them told me I would never be able to have a child.

My husband still loved me, but he desperately wanted a child, which is a must for us in our culture. If a woman can't give her husband a child, she becomes 'second hand.' My lovely husband wouldn't abandon me, but he talked about having a second wife for him to have a child. He would still keep me as his

first wife, love me, and take care of me. I was devastated and cried out to God for healing. Then you came to my village, and every day, I ran forward for prayer, wanting you to lay hands on me and pray personally for me among all the people, but you didn't.

The last day of your crusade came, and I told God, if the evangelist doesn't lay hands on me and pray for me, I will grab his trousers, and it worked!

"Sometime after the crusade, I fell ill and, hoping it would pass, I didn't do anything about it. Instead of getting better, it got worse, and my husband took me to the doctor at the hospital. After running all the tests, the doctor smiled and told me I wasn't sick at all, and a miracle had happened. I was pregnant with this boy I am holding in my arms right now."

What a glorious moment of praise and worship when all the people gave thanks to our God for His mercy and grace.

Then I asked for the baby boy's name, and again, this lady smiled and said, "Since we got our son from your ministry, we decided to call him Egon."

No, no, he doesn't look like me; he doesn't have my nose, ears, eyes, or skin color. God does not need my help. I am just His servant and messenger; He is the savior and healer!

I have lost count of the children in Tanzania named after me, but they are many.

WHERE IS MY BABY?

The local government of Mpanda joined the pastors who organized the crusade, and everybody expected something extraordinary to take place.

The crowd was packed on the crusade ground, and the Holy Spirit was moving mightily every day.

During the testimony time, after praying and ministering to the people, a very excited lady testified how she was blind, but during prayer, the Lord touched her and healed her. Now she was able to see everything clearly.

Suddenly, her hands went to her back, and she began to cry very loudly, almost screaming, "Where is my baby; where is my baby? When I came forward for prayer, my little baby was on my back, but she is not here now," and again, she cried out, "where is my baby?"

In Africa, all babies are tied orderly to the back of their mothers. I told the lady if she had her baby on her back when she came forward for prayer, I would find her baby, and suddenly, some of our crew came with the baby. When the mother took the baby in her arms, she began crying out of control, and when I asked her, why are you crying, Jesus just healed you and opened your eyes; you can see, and you should be happy.

I will never forget her answer, "I can feel with my hands that this is my baby, but I have never been able to see her; she is so beautiful!" Then I began to cry; it was a holy, touching moment.

CAN OLD PEOPLE GET HEALED?

Often, people think that elderly people can't get healed. Since you are old, you have to be sick and weak. People believe that's a part of life when you get old; anyhow, you will die soon.

I have seen many old people in Africa get healed, and one of them was an old, blind grandpa. His little grandson helped him get to the crusade, and when I gave the altar call, he guided him to the front for prayer.

Another gentleman, who was a witch doctor before he got saved, came to my crusade to check out if Jesus really can heal difficult cases, and when he saw this old and blind grandpa, he followed and watched him closely.

As we were praying for the masses of people with great needs, this old, blind grandpa shouted, "I can see. I am healed; I can see!"

The former witch doctor who came to investigate was surprised, but his life was changed from that moment. Later, he joined our Bible college in Arusha, and because he finished well, he became one of our most faithful coworkers until today.

A group of about 10 to 15 elderly people came walking with great difficulties and all with walking sticks to my crusade. Every day, we prayed for them, but nothing happened, and they limped and walked home again.

One day, I called them all to my stage, and some of them needed help to get up the steps.

Then, I prayed for them and demanded that they give me their walking sticks. No, no, they shouted, we can't walk home without our walking sticks. I asked them if they believed Jesus could heal them, and all of them answered with a big YES! I then grabbed all their walking sticks and told them to walk in Jesus' name! I even helped some of them by holding their hands, and suddenly, all of them, yes, all of them began to walk freely, and many of them danced for the Lord.

It was a great joy watching them walk home after the meeting fast and freely like young people.

Abraham was almost 100 years old, and his wife Sarah 90 years. Sarah was barren and unable to have a child, but when God showed up, Isaac, the son of God's promise, was born.

YES, ELDERLY AND OLD PEOPLE CAN GET SAVED AND HEALED.

THE TEST AT THE LOO.

Daniel from Kondoa was blind, and his brother had to help him with everything in his daily life, and it wasn't easy. So, when I came to Kondoa for a crusade, Daniel's brother brought Daniel to the crusade ground.

Daniel got healed, and when I checked him out, I knew it was a miracle.

Walking home that night with his brother, Daniel was so happy, but his brother doubted the miracle, and they started arguing. When they got home, Daniel needed to go to the toilet, and usually, his brother had to help him because a toilet in Africa can be very dark, and it can even be difficult for a seeing person to "hit" that little hole in the floor.

Usually, Daniel's brother helped Daniel because he had to

clean up after him if he went to the toilet by himself. Now, to settle their argument over the miracle, Daniel told his brother NOT to help or guide him at all. Daniel's brother was watching with skepticism when Daniel did his "business" and perfectly hit the right spot, and from that moment, his brother became a believer.

A DRUNK SOLDIER IN MAGU.

Why this former soldier, who was very drunk and could hardly walk straight, was allowed to enter my stage, I didn't know at that very moment, and I thought I would try to do the best I could with the situation.

"Who are you?" I asked him. The crowd laughed.

"I am a former soldier," he answered. He had difficulty speaking, and his smell was unbearable. He was unbelievably dirty and hadn't seen water and soap for a long time.

"You don't know why I am drunk; alcohol has destroyed my life," he said, and the people who knew him very well were still laughing.

"When Tanzania was at war with Uganda and chasing the dictator, Idi Amin, I was on the frontline, and I have killed so many people. All the time, their staring eyes are looking at me, day and night. I can't get a break or peace in my mind, and that's why I

began to drink alcohol. Now, my life is destroyed, but today, when you prayed for all the people, I prayed too and received Jesus as my Savior and Lord, and inside me, I felt a strong power hitting me. Now, even though I am drunk, I have peace in my mind and my heart."

People didn't believe him, and that was understandable. They had known him for years and even tried to help him without any results at all.

The next day, a nicely dressed gentleman came to my stage at the time of testimony, and I almost did not recognize him. It was the drunk soldier from yesterday. Now, he was a new person, born again with the power of the Gospel. He was cleaned up inside and outside. He wasn't an alcoholic anymore. Now, he spoke clearly, and the people didn't laugh at him; now, they were praising and worshipping the living God.

Abdallah, a Muslim from Nzega, hated my preaching, and he didn't attend the crusade at the crusade ground, but the message went all the way to his house because of my powerful P.A. system.

Now, he was standing drunk at my stage and telling the thousands of people how much he hated my preaching.

"Today," he said, "I left my house and went over to the other side of town, knowing I was far enough away not to hear you preach, but still, I couldn't get rid of your preaching. I went into a bar to escape, but inside this bar, I could hear you. I began to drink and got drunk, but you just continued to preach, and when you prayed for people, I felt a power I never felt before. It was like an explosion inside me, and now I know Jesus is my Savior and Lord.

"Dr. Egon," he said, "I want a new name. I don't want to be called Abdallah anymore; please, give me a new name. There and then, I gave him a new name and called him Emmanuel—it means "God with us!"

Instantly, Abdallah's drunkenness lifted, and he became a sober Emmanuel.

PLEASE DON'T TELL THEM THE WHOLE TRUTH.

The demonic world is real, and so are the witch doctors who many people fear. It's incredible the power some of those witch doctors have. It happened in the Bible days, and it's still happening.

At one crusade in the town of Kigoma at the shore of the beautiful Lake Tanganyika, I was interviewing a witch doctor who was delivered from many demons and gave her life to Jesus. Suddenly, in the middle of the big crowd, another witch doctor reacted very strongly and violently. My people had to bring her under control, but it was a difficult job, and finally, they carried her across the stage to a safe corner. Just as they passed me and the former witch doctor, who was testifying, the demons loudly screamed, "Don't tell them the whole truth!"

The devil and his demons know who Jesus is, and they know the truth as well. The demons don't want you to know the truth, and they do everything they possibly can to stop people from knowing the truth.

A witch doctor from Dar Es Salaam was trained by the Muslims and sent to the Arabic world for further training. This woman attended my crusade and surrendered her life to Jesus, and all the demons had to leave.

She brought all the stuff she used when she operated in the demonic world. My whole stage was covered with ugly stuff. Everything about demons is ugly and never nice and beautiful. You have to get rid of demonic stuff, and in my crusades, we always burn it.

Several witch doctors who got saved in my crusades are today serving God as ministers of the Gospel.

In 2008, when we planted our New Life City Church in Arusha, the Muslims sent witch doctors to infiltrate our people, hindering our church. Some of those people were possessed by many demons, and we had several situations where it looked like a warzone. All of them surrendered their lives to Jesus, and as always, the devil is a loser!

People ask me if I am afraid of demons, and my answer is always no, I am not.

On several occasions, demons have tried to kill me but always failed. Demons can't do me any harm because I am in Christ, born again and under the blood of Jesus.

Witch doctors from all over Tanzania have come together, cursed me, thrown ugly stuff after me, and even sent me letters.

They expected me to die, but on one occasion, I know the witch doctor died himself.

Never play with the demonic powers and the satanic demons. If you don't know what you are doing and if your life is not right with God, the satanic powers and demons will play with you.

Chapter Twelve

THE IMPOSSIBLE BECOMES POSSIBLE

Healed of HIV/AIDS - and resurected from the dead...

Too many people in Africa with HIV/AIDS have died a terrible and horrifying death without care, love, or medication.

I have been in those huts, in dark rooms, looking into their eyes, speaking hope, and praying God's love over a hopeless situation.

No medication or dirty tricks from witch doctors can heal people with HIV/AIDS, but Jesus is the best medication and healer.

I would never ever manipulate sick people by giving them false hope of being healed or getting better. Still, I have recognized that the greatest miracles happen when you preach the Gospel as Jesus said in Mark 16:17-18, "These signs will accompany those who believe: In my name, they will drive out demons; they will speak in new tongues, they will pick up snakes with their hands; and they will drink deadly poison, it will not hurt them at all: they will place their hands on sick people, and they will get well."

HIV/AIDS.

If you have been in an African hut made of grass and mud without electricity and water, looking into the desperate eyes of a dying person, dying from AIDS without a doctor or any medication to take away the pain, you understand that the "wages of sin is death!"

Many people are dying this terrifying, painful death without any hope and are forgotten by society. I visited a man in an African hut, lying in a cold dark room. Looking into his deep and fearful eyes, he told me, "If I knew the pain would be this terrible, I would never have been unfaithful to my wife." Words can't explain that feeling of hopelessness in the midst of a family with a wife and seven to nine children. Life has to continue, but how? In the darkest moment before entering into death and judgment of your sin, I am glad I know the gift of God, which is eternal life in Christ Jesus our Lord. Rom 6:23.

In the Southern part of Tanzania, we prayed for a younger guy with HIV/AIDS, and the doctors didn't give him any hope of surviving the disease. Before we prayed for him, he showed us the doctors' documents, and I understood the seriousness of the situation. Praying and believing God for a life-miracle, I told him to go back to the doctors for another test. At the hospital, he had to insist and beg the doctors to test him again.

The doctors told him, "You are wasting your money. You are dying from HIV/AIDS, and you don't have any chance of getting healed. You have to accept it and go home and prepare to die." This guy wouldn't give up hope and told the doctors he believed Jesus had healed him and he had the money to pay for another test.

The doctors ran the tests several times and couldn't believe the results; all HIV/AIDS was gone!

I will never forget when this guy showed up at the crusade with the hospital's documents proving the miracle.

Yes, with God, everything is possible even today.

In the city of Bukoba, a born-again, spirit-filled, faithful Christian woman was carried to my crusade. Three men who hated the Christians and the church had violently raped this woman to destroy her and her family and mock the church. It's unbelievable what the haters of Jesus can do; it's so evil. This woman had been in and out of the hospital. No one gave her any hope for survival; she was just skin over bone, and she was dying. She cried uncontrollably, and it was so unfair. She was clinging to dear life, having a husband and children. She was crying, why, God, why? As I ministered to her, I felt the pain, and I also felt very helpless.

Now, it was Sunday evening and the last day of the crusade, and as I for the last time ministered and prayed for this lady, I felt the power of healing so strongly.

I told her to go to the hospital the next morning with her pastor and ask for another test.

The next morning, we began our trip back home to Arusha, which was a two-day drive. After driving for about seven hours, my mobile phone rang. It was the woman's pastor, and he couldn't control his feelings and excitement. He shouted, "Dr. Egon, we have been at the hospital for hours. The doctors have repeatedly done all the tests. Finally, they surrendered, telling us something very unusual must have happened to this woman because she is completely healed and well."

RAISED FROM THE DEAD.

I had a co-worker for several years, but he became my co-worker only after his death. Yes, I know it sounds bizarre, but it's the truth.

This brother was from a poor family and lived a simple life in the village. He fell ill, and after some time, he died. The family and church members dogged his grave and laid out some dry grass on the floor of the grave. They didn't use a casket because of the lack of money but bought some white material to cover his body. When the body was laid to rest on the floor, they began to cover the body with soil, and suddenly, everybody was shocked. He, the dead man, began to cough. No, this is not fantasy; it really happened. They got him out of the grave, alive and well, and sometime after that, he became my co-worker.

Every funeral Jesus attended, he interrupted and destroyed, yes, even his own.

THE MAYOR OF CHATO.

Driving into Chato, we received the greatest welcome ever. Along with the local pastors, the Honorable mayor cleared the bus station and marketplace right in the middle of town because of our arrival. A big stage with two big chairs, one for me and one for Hannah, together with a lot of decorations, signaled something great was going to happen in Chato, and that was our crusade.

Through the P.A. system, the mayor welcomed us to his city and paid us great respect. Suddenly, I heard him tell the people to "Bring all the sick people to the crusade, bring them in cars, on motorbikes, bicycles, or wheelbarrows, for Dr. Egon will heal them

all tomorrow."

I jumped out of my big chair and shouted, "No, no, no, Sir, not me, but Jesus will heal the sick."

He looked at me and said, "No, you will heal the sick."

I answered, "No, I can't heal the sick."

He interrupted me and said, "I saw you heal one crippled woman crawling on all fours in Biharamulo some years ago. I know you can heal the sick people."

I remembered this crippled woman in Biharamulo. She had rubber on her hands, knees, and feet to protect her skin as she crawled on the streets. She was never able to stand up nor walk a single step.

This crippled woman came one evening, and as we were praying, the power of God hit her; she stood up and began to walk. She even walked up the steps to my stage and came toward me, jumping and dancing.

The crowd turned wild in worship to Jesus, and my government guest, the Honorable District Commissioner, grabbed my microphone and announced that the crusade would continue one more week.

The next day in Chato, people brought all their sick friends and family members with them on any kind of transportation possible.

After preaching the Gospel and leading people into salvation, we always pray for the sick and demon-possessed. In Chato, people were healed as Jesus promised, and even patients at the local hospital in their beds were healed and came to the crusade ground to testified to the glory of Jesus.

THE WITCH DOCTOR WHO DIED.

Witchcraft in many different forms is a big reality in the African culture, and it can be very powerful and scary.

In the Bible, we read a lot about witchcraft as well, and it goes far back in history.

I did a crusade in the town of Katesh, and we experienced the power of the Holy Spirit. Rumors went to the town of Mbulu, where the next crusade was scheduled. Many people in Mbulu were happy for the news of the upcoming crusade, but not the witch doctors in the area, and after doing all their "black magic," they sent one witch doctor to the town of Katesh to stop me from coming to their town, Mbulu, by killing me through witchcraft.

During the crusade in the town of Katesh, I gave an altar call and invited people to come forward down to the front of my platform. Hundreds of people responded, and the area was packed with people reaching out for God to save and heal them.

After the prayer, I always ask people to lift their hands and worship God in thanksgiving for all he has done for them. Among those people was the witch doctor from the town of Mbulu, and in his hand, he had some ugly "stuff" which he was supposed to throw and hit me with as I invited people to lift their hands. He lifted his hand in the air, and by the power of Jesus, his hand froze. He couldn't throw the "stuff," which was cursed with the evil powers to kill me. The power of God knocked him down on the ground. Our people and some local pastors picked him up, took him to a more private place, and ministered to him. Suddenly, the pastors realized that they couldn't get him back to life, and they rushed him to the hospital. When the medical doctor examined him, he suddenly opened his eyes and told the whole story of how he was supposed to kill me. Suddenly, he cried out, "The curse and spirit of death are coming back to me," and there and then, he died.

I am not happy about the witch doctor's death, but he had his chance to get right with God, and he decided not to.

We never play games with evil spirits, and we never experiment with the demons, but as Jesus said, "Cast them out!"

Chapter Thirteen

DR. EGON FALK - THE FISHERMAN OF PEOPLE

By Pastor Gunnar Jeppestøl

What was it that caused Egon, the son of a fisherman from the small village Tejn on the island of Bornholm, to become one of the biggest fishers of men in Africa?

Jesus must have recognized something in this young boy who said yes to the calling from Jesus to come and follow him. There was something on his heart, a passion for the lost. Jesus wanted to use him for something bigger than fish in the sea. He wanted to make him a fisher of men. I have seen this since I came to Tanzania for the first time to help teach at the seminars during the crusades. This was a man who had visions to reach the multitudes, someone who used a trawl. It was when Jesus saw the disciples letting out the trawl into the sea that he called them to become fishers of men. Dr. Egon is such a man with a big vision who let out the

For 32 years Gunnar Jeppestøl was the pastor of one of Norways biggest pentecostal churches, Filadelfia Vennesla.

trawl in the big sea of men in Tanzania. He is a man who is totally dedicated and consumed by the call Jesus has given to him. He has the desire to see at least 75 % of Tanzania's population saved!

It does not sound possible, but when we look at Tanzania today, it is possible. Since back to 1974, Dr. Egon and his wife, Hannah, have been faithful toward the calling and brought in the harvest for the Kingdom of God, more and more every year, thousands and thousands. What has impressed me the most is the strategic planning with crusades and seminars. They don't just go to the bigger cities, but they go to region after region and plan the crusades at the most central and strategic places to reach the whole area with the Gospel. They also organize, so the Christians can come and receive Bible teaching, both in the crusades and in the seminars in the mornings. The whole nation is covered.

When Dr. Egon enters the platform at the crusade, he has the whole crowd in his hand. He is like "a fish in the water." He speaks their own language, Swahili. He uses himself; he paints Jesus for their eyes. He uses humor, and he is serious, and the crowd receives his message. He reaches into their hearts with the message of Jesus. The Holy Spirit uses Dr. Egon as an instrument to reach the multitudes. The experience I have is that he belongs to the Tanzanian people; he just has another skin color. It's amazing to watch thousands after thousands stay in the hot afternoon sun and just listen to the Gospel while the evening and darkness are coming. It's just as we read in the Bible when Jesus came to Capernaum. "At evening, when the sun had set, they brought to Him all who were sick and those who were demon-possessed. And the whole city was gathered at the door.

Then he healed many who were sick with various diseases and cast out demons; and He did not allow the demons to speak, because they knew Him." Mark 1:32-34.

This could as well be the story of Dr. Egon's crusades from somewhere in Tanzania.

It's the ministry of Jesus, which continued with the disciples, and it's taken further when Dr. Egon preaches and draws in the big Gospel trawl full of precious people. They run to the platform when Dr. Egon calls for salvation and a new life. It's evident that Jesus gets their hearts. People cry, laugh, and are filled with joy when they experience the Gospel's power.

After the salvation prayer, the prayer for the sick people begins. Many times, the demon-possessed people have already manifested at this point, with their screams and violent behavior, just as we read in the Bible when Jesus had his crusade.

It's absolutely important to have the gift of God to be able to preach in these crusades, where so many people do not know the Gospel or the Bible.

Without this special calling and this gift, you will never reach the multitudes.

We see how Jesus is doing amazing miracles and wonders, which confirm the Word of God. Every night, we experience how the blind can see, the deaf can hear, the lame can walk, and demon-possessed people are set free. It's the Acts of the Apostles that continue.

The apostle Paul also talked about signs and wonders through evangelism.

Rom: 15,19, "In mighty signs and wonders, by the power of the Spirit of God" It's a necessary part for the Gospel to break through.

I knew it was true when I heard that some enemies of the Gospel did not want three people in Tanzania. They were Dr. Egon Falk, Evg. Reinhard Bonnke, and Evg. Aril Edvardsen.

I believe that the way Dr. Egon organizes his work with crusades, seminars, and the Bible school Academy of Leadership in Arusha is the best and most successful way to evangelize in Tanzania.

I have a lot of respect for Dr. Egon and Hannah Falk, who have worked since 1974 in Tanzania. They get into their vehicle and drive where there are almost no roads, only dusty and bumpy roads. They drive in extreme heat, far away from their family and a welfare that we take for granted.

It is amazing to experience them meeting with the pastors again and again for another crusade with the same enthusiasm and fire for the Gospel.

Week after week, year after year, they contain a burning fire of love for Jesus and the people of Tanzania.

When they are not in a crusade, they tend to different works at the home office. They have a home for disadvantaged children, children's schools, a Bible school Academy of Leadership, and they give humanitarian help to many people.

When they are not in Tanzania, they will travel to other places in the world and raise financial support for the next crusade. New areas

must be reached with the Good News about Jesus Christ—the only hope for the world!

Chapter Fourteen
THE CHILDREN OF MY HEART
Verner from Kibondo and the others...

When I see handicapped and sick children, it always touches my heart, and I want to help them to a better future.

| Egon greets a little African boy.

I will never forget when two men carried this boy called Verner, hanging from their hands as they lifted him by his arms to my platform during prayers.

Everything from Verner's stomach and down was only skin and bone without any life in it.

Verner was about five or six years old and born lame like this. He lived with his elderly grandparents, and life wasn't good at all.

My people left Verner behind me on my platform at the feet of a visiting pastor friend from Norway, Gunnar Jeppestol. What could he do? He began to pray for Verner, and suddenly, I heard a joyful noise behind me, and when I turned around and looked, I saw Verner on his feet, walking toward me with a great big smile on his pretty face.

In the beginning, his walking wasn't stable, but with every step, he improved and became stronger and stronger.

When I asked if anyone knew Verner, the Anglican priest came forward and recognized this boy as Verner, and in shock, he

shouted, "He can't walk. He has never been able to stand on his feet."

Then Verner's grandpa showed up, and in amazement, he couldn't believe what had just happened to his grandson.

He told the crowd that he and his wife had cared for Verner since he was born and all the hardships they had experienced, and then he said, "I left Verner behind me at home, not believing in any future for my grandson. I even don't know who brought him to the crusade meeting."

Then they walked home together!

A BOY NAMED RUBEN.

A poor and heavily pregnant woman walked from her village to the hospital to give birth but never made it there. She and her husband couldn't afford to pay for any transportation.

Can you imagine being heavily pregnant and walking mile after mile in the African heat under the burning sun on a dusty road being in labor? She did but missed the hospital by some few miles. She was tired and worn out and fell into a ditch not far from my crusade ground and gave birth to a baby boy, and then she died.

People on the road took her and the little newborn to the hospital, but the doctors couldn't do anything for the mother, and she was declared dead.

That night, after dinner and during our devotion, the head nurse came into our dining room and asked us to pray for this little boy who was very weak and sick. As we held this little one in our arms, Mr. Vino, who was our missionary doctor working with us in New Life Outreach, whispered in my ear that all the internal organs in this little boy's body didn't function at all, and he was dying in our arms.

What could we do other than cry out to our Lord Jesus? And I tell you, so we did! Believing and trusting God for a miracle, we handed the little baby boy over to the head nurse again. Every time I woke up that night, I thought about that baby boy and thanked God for a miracle, and the next morning, at our breakfast, the head nurse showed up with this little one in her arms with a big smile on her face. He was not only alive, but all his internal organs functioned perfectly, and he was full of life.

The head nurse asked us to give this newborn miracle boy a name, and since our son, Ruben H. Falk was there together with us, we named him Ruben.

Ruben stayed at the hospital's orphanage for two years, and after that, he was handed over to his father, who, by now, was able to take care of him.

Ruben will forever be in my heart!

CHILDREN.

Jesus showed his love for children during his time of ministry, and we should do the same.

When children suffer from lack of food or disease, sickness or lack of love and care, my heart breaks into a thousand pieces. Children are hidden away because they were born with defects and not-so-normal bodies, being misused, abused, and looked down at with hateful eyes. I see the fear and hurt in the faces of these little ones.

Again and again, I have seen angels caring for these little children as Jesus brings them healing, deliverance, and peace. So many times, I have seen hurting and crying mothers bringing their children for prayer during my crusades, and I have witnessed the greatest miracles happen to these little ones.

Can I ever forget the beautiful little baby girl, nicely dressed up in the arms of her crying mother? NO, I CAN'T!

This little girl was also born with the male private part, and for the parents, it was a shameful thing, and they didn't know what to do until I came preaching the Good News.

After prayer, the mother of the baby girl and my wife Hannah went to a private area behind my stage and checked and found out the male part was gone, and the baby girl was 100% girl.

Another baby was born with a hole in her neck. When she got milk from her mother, it ran out again through the hole.

They lived in a small village with no doctors or hospitals, so now they came into the town of Sengerema because they had heard about a specialist doctor from Europe helping children with defects.

When they came to Sengerema and were on their way to the hospital, they heard my preaching and stopped to check me out. By the Word and the Holy Spirit, they were captivated and brought their baby forward for prayer, and as we were praying, right there in front of our eyes, Doctor Jesus did the surgery and closed the hole. It just happened instantly, and can you imagine how happy and thankful the parents were?

They canceled their visit to the specialist doctor at the hospital and returned home with great joy.

Many poor children get a good start in life through New Life's schools.

Chapter Fifteen
THE SMELL OF AFRICA

By Nick Hansen, Chairman of the Board of New Life Outreach DK.

Standing on the stage for the first time looking out on the crowd of thousands of faces,

some ecstatic with anticipation, others wondering what is going on, as the worship team sings and plays festive songs of worship. The dust rises from the ground as people dance and rejoice in the dry market square in the afternoon sun. The worship leader sings a line in Swahili and the crowd happily repeats him, and so this goes on for hours.

Nick Hansen, Chairman of the Board in New Life Outreach, Denmark.

I am 20 years old, freshly out of school, and just landed in central Tanzania. I am overwhelmed by the strong sunlight and heat, contrasting with the dark, cold Denmark I just left five days ago as a winter-pale young man embarking on his emancipatory rite as far away from home as possible, doing his version of the aborigines' walkabout.

The smells—oh, the unmistakable smell of Africa—one moment, a whiff of a warm, full garbage can and cadavers, then the smell of lime soap, the next moment the smell of cumin, cardamom, cinnamon, and garlic from the small outdoor kitchens as the ladies prepare pilau for supper. But dirt, mostly dry, sunbaked dirt, is the smell of this fierce warrior woman named Africa. I am taking it in, hating it, and loving it. But she has me in her grip; I am falling in love with this nation.

Looking back on this young lad that is me over 25 years ago, I can honestly say I saw how God is a great God. That season of my life changed my whole understanding of Jesus today and shaped my life. It propelled me into ministry, and I owe Doctor Egon and Mama Hannah so much. Today, I am a part of the New Life Outreach board because of what Tanzania did to me back then.

In this chapter, I will share parts of my diary, so you may be able to see through the eyes of a young Scandinavian kid, hardly worth calling a man.

January 17th, 1994, Hannah and Egon Falk are visiting my parents because they are good friends and want to spend a cozy day together. My mother had planted the idea of me going with them to Africa a couple of days before. Now, as they are here, it suddenly becomes real. The decision is made, and only two days later, I have a ticket in my hand and red marks on my shoulders and butt cheek from the vaccinations against hepatitis and a bunch of other stuff.

I meet Hannah and Egon at the Copenhagen airport. After a typical journey in a hot, confined metal tube 30,000 feet above ground, we land in Nairobi, Kenya on Friday morning.

A little late, a white and red Toyota pickup arrives with New Life Outreach's logo written on the sides. Out of the car steps two young men; behind the wheel is Torstein, a young 22-year-old Norwegian, white hair and very tanned. He reminds me of a white African farmer. On the other side of the car steps out a slightly older German man named Jürgen; he is very talkative and looks like Africa is his home turf. Now starts a four-hour drive to Arusha in Tanzania.

It's like watching a nature program on TV; the whole journey is one long safari, long roads with a view of beautiful dry landscapes and exotic animals like zebras, giraffes, and even a dead elephant, bloated and ready to burst. Despite the air conditioning, the car is sweltering, and I wonder why I'm not more baffled and amazed by this whole new civilization I just landed in.

On the ride, Torstein sits behind the wheel, quiet and calm, and he is navigating to avoid the potholes in the road at full speed. Jürgen, on the other hand, is very talkative as he is trying to update Hannah and Egon on what has happened and what the current situation is. Finally, the car reaches Arusha, and the first stop is the mission camp base. Here, I meet the missionary Bjarke for the first time, sitting in the shade in a peculiar position that turns out to be his favorite whenever he relaxes.

I get introduced to many people whose names I quickly forget, but they are so excited to see Doctor Egon returning to their nation. Mama Hannah is tired and has no food in the house, so we go out to eat instead, and only a few minutes later, we are downtown in the only pizzeria in town. I am reminded that I had asked her before we drove out of Nairobi how big the city of Arusha is, to which she replied it was not as big as the capital, Nairobi. In comparing the two cities, this must be the understatement of the year. Arusha is basically one long paved street with small side streets hardly drivable.

We drive to the Falk family home, three miles outside the city and only a few hundred feet from the main street. It is a beautiful house that is a mix of colonial building style and Danish interior design, just as I like it. As I step out of the car, four guard dogs come and size me up; the German Shepherds approve and leave. They do not like strangers, but they step aside when the owner is home. I meet the night guards and the housekeeper, who has tended the house in the Falks' absence.

Saturday morning, we are going to the downtown market to buy groceries, rice, fruit, and vegetables. I must laugh; this is supposedly the biggest and best marketplace in the nation. Oh, my little white head is spinning; is this really the best? Afterward, we drive to the local supermarket called Kibo. Again, I am laughing. When the mental image is something like Walmart, entering a 300-square-foot room packed with all kinds of things is a different experience. All over the place, I see stacks of lime soap. I can smell it, the same smell as in the airport as I set foot on the African continent.

Sunday morning, I go to church with Egon. We persuade Bjarke to join us, but he only wants to come on one

condition: he will not go up to the pulpit. He is not in Tanzania to preach but to support the ministry with practical work. As we leave for church, Torstein, Jürgen, and the rest of the team drive the big trucks out to set up for the next evangelistic crusade.

It is great to be in an African Sunday service; Bjarke and I sit as far back as possible to ensure Bjarke will not be brought up on stage. It is hot; it is sultry; it is loud. Everybody is sitting or standing very close in the big auditorium, and in the two or three hours the meeting lasts, I am sitting, forced to have my nose stuck in the armpit of my sweaty neighbor. Here, smell is not an issue. If you break wind, no problem; it is only frowned upon if you can hear it.

I don't understand much of the meeting, but the worship in Swahili is intoxicating. I know that part, regardless of the language. The rhythm, music, and singing are delightful, and I feel totally at home as everybody raises their voice, singing alleluia to the melody of Amazing Grace.

It is Monday morning, my fourth day in a strange land. Bjarke, who is a carpenter by trade, asks me to help him fix a house. Quickly, I learn two things. 1) my head knowledge might be good, but in Africa, it is all about the hands. I had come with my bright mind, knowing the formulas for electricity, mass and space, and several languages. But my hands are as delicate as tender veal, never having been more stressed than when I had an after-school job as a cleaning assistant at a nursing home. This is my wake-up call. I am close to useless unless I find something to make myself helpful. 2) My initial thought is that the Falk family lives very comfortably compared to the rest of the local society. But quickly, I learn that when you're in a foreign culture, far away from your family and roots, it is essential to have something that functions and where you can be yourself and find contentment.

Tuesday morning at 5:00, one hour before the sun rises, we are up and getting ready to drive out to the big crusade. As the sun wakes, we are riding out of town on roads toward the village Kilosa, 400 miles away. Thanks to the enormous expressive giftings, Egon is generous in sharing his ministry knowledge, which makes it very rewarding and informative and not the least boring on the long ride. It could have been a drag, but Egon is not afraid to share good and funny stories of what he has experienced.

Being a Dane, you can't help but feel a bit proud since Danish contractors are building the big paved roads in most of Tanzania, paid for by Danish aid, which is why they are called "the roads of the Danes." Once you've driven on the uneven dirt roads for hours, getting back on the highway feels like flying. That makes most of our ride fairly easy, but still, after many hours of driving, my bum gets a bit tired and my legs stiff.

In the late afternoon, we finally arrive at our destination; it feels like having reached the end of the world. Could there really be a village in the middle of this no man's land? We quickly find the place where the stage and the big loudspeaker towers have been erected. It looks like some sort of marketplace or sports arena. Egon tells me that he does not like the walls surrounding the place; it might prevent

people from attending. We ask for directions and get to the place where the big containers, refitted for living, are parked. Egon notices they are parked in the shade; otherwise, they would be unbearably hot to live in. One container is where he and Hannah live. The other young missionaries and I stay in the other container that is also transformed into a cozy place for us during the Crusades.

Usually, Hannah is on the Crusades, preparing food for all the white missionaries, who are not that keen on Tanzanian food, just like the Tanzanian workers do not fancy European food. Everybody just wants their mama's food; that is the way it is, and that is fine. But this time, Hannah is not there, so I get to eat local Tanzanian food. As we sit, a lady brings a water dish and soap so we can wash our hands. And after that, we are served ugali, rice, meat stew (I think it's goat meat floating in fat). We use our hands when we eat. No utensils. In addition, mango, banana, soda, and coffee are served. That is the food every day. You do not need to be in Africa for long to discover that the meals are the highlight of the day; you spend at least an hour on lunch and an hour on dinner, and at least half an hour on breakfast. There is no rush when it comes to eating. This is the time where good stories of what has happened are shared. Laughter and fun are the keys to good food.

Wednesday, the crusade begins. People come from everywhere, and as the music starts playing, more and more arrive. Just yesterday, it seemed like a small village with only a few hundred people, but now thousands are gathering. The loudspeakers are blasting out worship many miles away, drawing people to come. After a couple of hours of music, singing, and performance by the local church choir, Doctor Egon gets up on the pulpit and starts to preach. He is keeping his audience riveted, telling stories of what Jesus has done. After 45 minutes of sharing the gospel, he calls people to Salvation; hundreds come up in front of the stage, maybe thousands. People are led in a prayer of Salvation; you can hear in their voices that this is significant, and this is real to them. Ushers walk around with small pieces of paper, asking people to register their information to get connected with a church afterward.

As I'm standing looking over the crowds of people surrendering their life to Christ, far away from Denmark, Europe, and the rest of the Western world, I'm reminded about the parable that Jesus tells. The Shepherd goes out to find that one sheep that is lost, leaving the 99 behind. Once it is found, he comes back, tells his neighbors to come and celebrate together with him, for the sheep that was lost has been found, and there is more rejoicing over the one that was lost but found than over the 99 that were never lost. So, it is in heaven as one soul turns to Christ. This is the gospel in a nutshell; this is what I see unfolding right in front of my eyes. I'm overwhelmed with the presence of God as people are surrendering their lives to Him, and I can see the change happening in their faces.

As I stand there, I'm not scared or bewildered, but I'm overwhelmed by the vast number of people who are coming to Christ. As soon as people have given their lives to Christ,

Egon immediately starts to pray for the sick. Just like hundreds, maybe thousands of people raised their hands to surrender their lives to Christ, now hundreds of hands are being raised to get prayed for to get miraculous healing. In a place where there is no hospital, no clinic, no doctor, there is only the great physician, Christ, to help people with their diseases. And as people pray, Jesus listens and heals. I am standing there stunned; Egon calls me to assist him in praying for people.

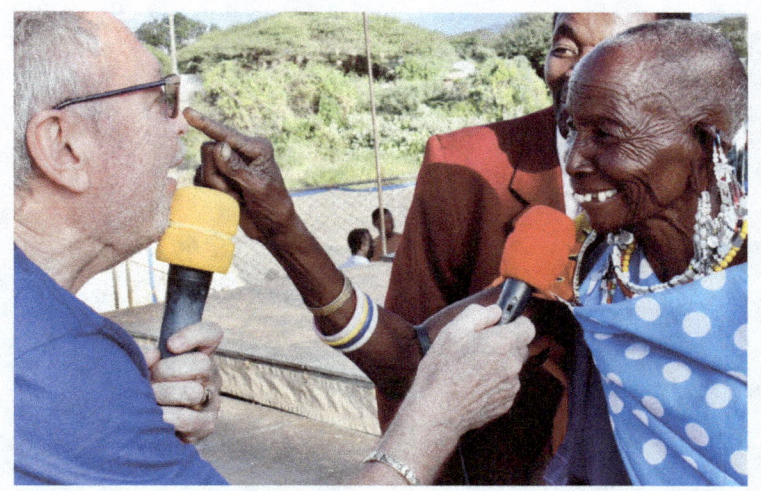

A blind woman has been healed at a campaign and gratefully shows that she can now see and point out Egon's nose.

As the team walks around and prays with people, we hear cries of joy as people experience the healing power of Christ. Soon, the stage is full of people who claim that they have just experienced miraculous healing. Families and friends are called to testify what the disease was like and what had happened during prayer. Time and time again, we see people who could not hear now able to hear, people who weren't able to see now seeing, people unable to speak now speaking, people unable to walk now walking. And this is just day one out of a whole week here.

I am grateful to have a journal that shows that I already have the power of God so clearly emphasized in my youth. Now, my story goes on, telling about all the adventures and discoveries I had during my stay in Tanzania. But think for a moment about this: what I saw that first crusade evening, Egon and his team have done hundreds of times before and since then. Since the foundation of New Life Outreach, over one million souls have been registered as giving their life to Christ. Think about that—

1,000,000. How many other ministries do you know that have done that?

Egon Falk preaches at a major campaign in Sudan.

This is truly a work of God and worthy of giving Him glory. I can only encourage you to support this ministry, as I can testify to the fruits of its labor. And I see that with a few dollars, we can do such great work. Not only is the gospel being received by many, but they are also receiving teaching in Bible school. In addition, children are put in regular schools, the hungry are fed, and orphans are given a home. All this through one man who dared to follow the calling of Christ in his life.

We are finally back in Arusha after weeks of back-to-back crusades in several places in central and northern Tanzania. Trucks and equipment are being fixed after being exposed to the sun's harshness, dust, and bumpy roads. The fast-paced days of crusades, with all the impressions of thousands of faces changed forever, have turned to a more somber and reflective time as we prepare for the next season. The seasonal rain in this region comes as showers once or twice a day, often as the sun sets, and then it goes on for a couple of hours. It is so brutal that we have to talk louder with one another. In the distance, I hear the sound of rushing water filling the riverbed. The violent rain has loosened big rocks from Mount Meru, which are rolling through the waters, sounding their presence with deep pounding bumps that are felt under my feet.

But tonight is a quiet evening. Yet again, Mama Hannah has made a lovely dinner for us, and the three of us are sitting around the table chatting and having fun. Suddenly, Egon's face changes character as he starts sharing their story with me. How he was called as a boy to speak to people with dark skin, how they moved their whole family to Tanzania in

'73, and just a couple of years later, went back deadly ill and with a crushed dream of reaching the African hearts with the gospel.

As he is talking, I am telling myself to listen carefully. These are God-given life lessons on what ministry and following Christ costs. Everything I hear is precious wisdom shared by a man who has proved the validity of his words. He then shares how God brought his dreams back to life and how God set up everything for a big and demanding vision. As Egon comes to a close, I express my gratitude and go to my room to pray and praise God for the gift of letting me know the principles, patterns, and divine structure that govern anyone who wants to follow Christ. I will do just like Mary and take it to heart and not forget the Lord's instructions. This is a defining night in my life.

As the evening rain starts pouring down, the temperature drops, and I put on a warm sweater. My mother had helped me pack for the trip and said it could get cold, which I didn't believe, and after being on the Crusades in 100° F midday sun, I believed it even less. Here I am, grateful for my mother's advice and the gray sweater that keeps me comfortable and warm. As the rain stops, I go out into the pitch-black night; everything is quiet, and the air is crisp and clean. I smell the wet soil that somehow connects me with mother earth; I am centered and grounded. My mind and heart have been changed; my body feels connected. The clouds disperse, and millions of stars twinkle as a greeting from heaven. It feels like a moment of destiny.

I now know the smell of Africa, the smell of heartfelt

worship, the smell of surrender to Christ. I understand that this nation has God's interest. "For we are to God the sweet aroma of Christ among those who are being saved and those who are perishing." (2 Cor. 2:15).

I am taking it in; I am falling in love with my God once again.

Looking back on how Tanzania has changed from being a Muslim nation with a few million inhabitants to 45 million in just a few decades, predominantly Christian, I see how New Life Outreach has been a central tool in this change for the good of the people. And coming back now, I hardly recognize the nation I visited for the first time in '94 as a young man. I am grateful to God for letting me be a small piece of that.

Today, my story has become the story of my own children, who, at a young age, followed in my footsteps to Tanzania to see the faces, experience the music, and smell the same things.

The plane is taking off, leaving Africa behind me as I go back to my own nation and family. I literally sit with the feeling that a part of my heart hasn't left the ground, and like a rubber band, my heart is being stretched further and further as the plane ascends. I cover my face and close my eyes as tears run down my cheeks.

I already miss her and her smell.

Chapter Sixteen
FOR GOD EVERYTHING IS POSSIBLE
Bring Dr. Egon back to laela.

Preaching the Gospel of Jesus Christ to the multitudes is my God-given calling and passion. Seeing people respond and receive salvation, the forgiveness of sin, and change is absolutely worth living for.

I was preaching in a small village in the Southern part of Tanzania where nobody else goes. There are no hotels, restaurants, running water, or electricity. The only heat is from the burning sun and lots of dust. I was hit with overwhelming passion when a small car drove up and "unloaded" a skeleton, a dying lady.

The doctors from a faraway hospital had called this lady's family, telling them to come and pick up the "body" because they couldn't do anything to help and save her life.

When the family members came to the hospital, they humbly asked the doctors to give her some painkillers and intravenous fluid for the long journey on the bumpy road home to Laela, their village. The doctors responded with a NO and said it's a waste of medicine and money since she is already "dead."

When I looked at this lady, she was only skin and bones. Her eyes were empty, and I couldn't recognize her breathing. For a moment, I felt so powerless. I called upon the name of Jesus and for the mercy of our Almighty God. I truly felt the loving arms of God touching us and the power of life entered into this powerless skeleton of skin and bones.

The crowd exploded and rejoiced in a way I can't explain. It was like all Heaven came down and rejoiced together with us.

Suddenly, so many healings took place all over, and it wouldn't stop when a crippled young man who had never walked was not only perfectly walking but running.

Every time and for a long time after the crusade, people shouted, "Bring Dr. Egon back," when they, in the streets of Laela, saw this young and former crippled man or this lady.

These people and many more are living and walking testimonies today, testifying to the greatness and love of our Savior, Jesus Christ.

It's nothing about me but everything about Jesus!

HIS WIFE DIDN´T RECOGNIZE HIM.

During my crusades, I always eat dinner with my team, and one night in Dar Es Salaam, the biggest city in Tanzania, it took longer than usual for the team to return to camp, and I wondered what was wrong. Finally, when the team arrived, all of them were so excited and flying high, and I had to tell them to calm down a bit.

Listen, they said, and all of them wanted to talk to me at the same time. After you left and we were closing down, a gentleman came forward and asked for you, but you were gone, and then he told his testimony.

This gentleman was totally crippled and came to the crusade yesterday, believing God for his miracle to take place. During the prayer for the sick people, God's power hit him and healed him from top to toe.

Later that evening, when he arrived at his house, his wife had locked the doors for security reasons, and he didn't bring any keys with him. When he knocked on the door, his wife opened the window and asked him, "Who are you?"

Since this gentleman always had been crippled, his wife didn't recognize him; she was scared and closed the window.

This gentleman had to bargain with his wife and explain what had happened, but she couldn't believe it. Finally, and fearfully, she opened the door and said, it's the voice of my husband but not the body.

That night, we had a praise meeting before we were able to eat dinner together.

SENTENCED TO 30 YEARS IN PRISON WITHOUT PAROLE.

One day, I was sitting in my office, reading a letter from a hard-core criminal who was put in jail for 30 years.

One of my small books had ended up in the prison and in the hands of this man. As he was reading the salvation prayer, something very powerful happened to him; he got saved.

I have read and heard people say that God doesn't act on people reading prayers, but I know God answered Frank's prayer when he honestly read the prayer from my book.

This guy asked me for Bibles and books, and over several years, we were connected and corresponded through letters.

Something very strange and powerful happened. The judge who sentenced Frank to 30 years in jail without parole suddenly, out of nowhere, remembered this hard-core criminal and wanted to know how he was doing. This is not a routine procedure at all, but for our Almighty God, it is.

When the judge got the result from the investigation, he was told that the guy he put behind bars was not the same hard-core criminal anymore, but he had changed until the guards couldn't recognize him.

Reading the facts of the investigation, the judge did something he never ever had done before, and after 11 years in prison, Frank was let out into freedom and a totally new life.

I didn't know what had happened to Frank, and one Sunday afternoon, my mobile phone rang, and it was Frank telling me the story. Then, he said, "By the way, Dr. Egon, right now I am together with a demon-possessed man. How can I cast out the demons?"

I told him what to do, meaning to cast them out in the name of Jesus. No dialog nor discussion but only command; cast them out, Jesus said, and then we hung up.

After about 45 minutes, Frank called me again, and with joy in his voice, he shouted, "It's working, Dr. Egon; the demons are gone, and the man is born again and saved!"

I invited Frank to my Bible college in Arusha and gave him a scholarship for one year, and he was a great student.

After finishing Bible school, he needed a job and applied to be the manager for one of the more prominent bus companies in Tanzania, and by the grace of God, he got the job.

One Sunday morning, I met him in our church, and, smiling from ear to ear, he told me that the job as a manager was too boring for him. He had a new exciting job as a leader for a security company, transporting big amounts of money from bank to bank or from businesses to banks. I had to contain myself, thinking about how "funny" God sometimes is; now, the hardcore criminal was guarding big money he earlier wanted to steal.

Today, Frank is serving God and planting churches.

THE THREE ROBBERS.

I was doing a crusade and seminar in a small village when three bandits from outside the village decided to rob us of our money and equipment. They checked everything out and decided first to steal our equipment from the church, where we did our teaching seminar. But that night, when they came to the church in the African darkness, they were met with an invisible force like a wall hindering them from entering the church building. Taken by surprise and not knowing what it was, they decided to go to the crusade site and steal as much as possible of our

valuable equipment. Again, coming close to our containers and stage, an invisible force like a wall stopped them, and they couldn't do anything.

Now, the three bandits were in a state of shock and didn't know what to do. After some time, they decided to go to my accommodations and rob my wife and me, but for the third time, this invisible force like a wall stopped them, and they were not able to move close to our accommodation containers.

They said that they came to this village to get something, so they decided to rob the first public bus out of the village in the morning. Outside the village, they blocked the road, and the bus had to stop. The bandits demanded that all the passengers strip naked and go on the roof of the bus. They did not know there was a police officer among the many passengers, and he attacked one of the bandits and knocked him out with an iron bar. Simultaneously, some other passengers got the second bandit, but the third one managed to escape.

During the Saturday night farewell dinner with the local pastors and government officials, the police chief told me the whole story. When I asked the police chief what would happen to the bandits, he said with a big smile, "Case closed!"

When he recognized that I didn't understand the meaning, he told me the bandits didn't survive the visit at the police station. Case closed!

DRIVING ON EMPTY TANKS.

It was difficult for some years to buy food, etc., in Tanzania, and all the shops were totally empty. Life was very hard and difficult, but God gave us the greatest miracles of all time.

Since it was impossible to buy bread, my wife Hannah baked bread—if we were able to get some flour. One day, we didn't have any more flour nor bread. Suddenly, my phone rang, and a gentleman asked me if we had any flour. When I told him we didn't, he told me to come quickly to his shop, and when I showed up, he gave me 200 kg of flour. There were a lot of bugs in the flour, but when we spread it out in the sun on a canvas, all the bugs marched away very quickly.

Another time, we didn't have any rice or cooking oil, and a truck just stopped in front of our house and unloaded a big sack of rice and a gallon of cooking oil. I didn't know the driver, and when I asked him why he dropped off all that rice and cooking oil, he answered that his boss told him to do so. His boss was a Muslim and lived in another part of the country.

Getting fuel for our vehicles was impossible. If you had luck, you got 30 liters from the government office, but I always had not less than 2000 liters in my storeroom.

My team with the big 18-wheelers and all the crusade equipment was on the way to one of my crusades. They needed to refuel a couple of hundred miles before reaching the crusade city. All our vehicle's tanks were almost empty, and they stopped in a small town and asked all over if they could buy some fuel, but the whole place was empty and dry. There was no way my team

could continue the journey because the last stretch before coming to the destination was without any gas stations and very much a desert area without cities.

The only thing my team could do was believe in God for a miracle. All the team members laid their hands on every fuel tank on the vehicles and prayed for a fuel miracle. Even though all the indicators showed empty, the drivers cranked the engines and began to drive—to pray and to drive. Now, the tanks were absolutely dried up, no more fuel, but the engines still worked, mile after mile, until they arrived at the destination and drove up in front of a gas station where they could buy fuel—and the engines stopped.

Did we have a fantastic crusade? Oh, yes, we did! God is still a God of creating miracles from the impossible, such as allowing us to drive on empty tanks.

Chapter Seventeen
THE ZANZIBAR CRUSADES

For centuries past, cardamom, clove, and cinnamon culled from the fabled spice gardens of the enchanted island of Zanzibar have been prized by sultans and princes alike.

Now, you can pick them for yourself on a spice tour that takes you from the winding alleys, carved doors, and cool courtyards of Stone Town, through the slave caches of the coral bays, past the blue-domed bathhouses of long-dead sultans, and out onto the silver and blue ribbons of Zanzibar's perfect beaches.

To enter the world of Zanzibar is to step through the looking glass into the world of a thousand and one nights and black eyes that smile from behind deep veils. There's a House of Wonders and a street of food, a Palace Museum, an ancient
slave market, an age-old fort, a ruined harem, and the house where Dr. Livingstone once lived.

There are Red Colobus Monkeys and dolphins and a bright tapestry of Arab, African, and Swahili culture, folklore, and cuisine that are as mesmerizing as myth.

There's also a wide selection of wonderful hotels, wide-open beaches, and all the facilities that you could possibly require.

FACT FILE:

- **Area:** Zanzibar 3,354 km, Pemba 1,537 km
- **Population:** 1,000,000 approximately
- **Language:** Kiswahili (English widely spoken)
- **Religion:** Predominantly Muslim with Christian and Hindu as a minority.
- **Capital:** The capital of Zanzibar, located on the island of Unguja, is Zanzibar City, and its old quarter, known as Stone Town, is a World Heritage Site. Zanzibar Town

ZANZIBAR.

The word "Zanzibar" probably derives from the Persian *Zangibar* ("coast of the blacks"); ultimately from the Arabic words of the same meaning. Once a separate state with a long trading history within the Arab world, Zanzibar united with Tanganyika to form Tanzania in 1964 and still enjoys a high degree of autonomy within the union.

Zanzibar's primary industries are spices, raffia, and tourism. It is still sometimes referred to as the Spice Islands (a term also associated with the Maluku Islands in Indonesia) because of the significance of its production of cloves, of which it used to be the world leader, and also nutmeg, cinnamon, and pepper.

The ecology is of note for being the home of the endemic Zanzibar Red Colobus and the elusive Zanzibar Leopard.

STONE TOWN.

The capital city, Zanzibar, is divided into two sections: Stone Town, a World Heritage site, and Ngambo. The buildings are predominantly white coral stone with a noticeable Arab architectural style. Balconies in Stone Town surround central courtyards and open-arched rooms to ensure that the interiors are always cool. The exterior doors are intricately carved and inlaid with brass.

Narrow roads meander between buildings, some over a century old, leading you to picturesque bazaars with carpenters, jewelers, hawkers, tailors, and coffee sellers. Along the island's eastern shore runs a protective reef, which is as beautiful as it is functional.

CULTURE.

Zanzibar is a conservative, Sunni Muslim society. Its history was influenced by the Arabs, Persians, Indians, Portuguese, British, and the African mainland.

Stone Town is a place of winding lanes, circular towers, carved wooden doors, raised terraces, and beautiful mosques. Important architectural features are the Livingstone house, the Guliani Bridge, and the House of Wonders. The town of Kidichi features the hammam (Persian baths), built by immigrants from Shiraz, Iran, during the reign of Barghash bin Said.

TRADE.

Zanzibar, mainly Pemba Island, was once the world's leading clove producer, but annual clove sales have since plummeted by 80% since the 1970s. Explanations given for this are a fast-moving global market, international competition, and a hangover from Tanzania's failed experiment with socialism in the 1960s and '70s when the government controlled clove prices and exports. Zanzibar now ranks a distant third, with Indonesia supplying 75% of the world's cloves, compared to Zanzibar's 7%.

Zanzibar exports spices, seaweed, and fine raffia. It also has a large fishing and dugout canoe production. Tourism is a major foreign currency earner.

HISTORY.

The presence of microlithic tools attests to 20,000 years of human occupation of Zanzibar. The islands became part of the wider world's historical record when Arab traders discovered them and used them as a base for voyages between Arabia, India, and Africa.

Unguja offered a protected and defensible harbor, so although the archipelago offered few products of value, the Arabs settled at what became Zanzibar City (Stone Town) as a convenient point from which to trade with East African coastal towns. They established garrisons on the islands and built the first mosque in the Southern hemisphere.

During the Age of Exploration, the Portuguese Empire was the first European power to gain control of Zanzibar and kept it for nearly 200 years. In 1698, Zanzibar fell under the control of the Sultanate of Oman, which developed an economy of trade and cash crops with a ruling Arab elite. Plantations were developed to grow spices, hence the moniker of the Spice Islands (a name also used of Dutch colony the Moluccas, now part of Indonesia). Another major trade good was ivory, the tusks of elephants killed in mainland Africa. The third pillar of the economy was slaves, giving Zanzibar an important place in the Arab slave trade,

the Indian Ocean equivalent of the better-known Triangular Trade. Zanzibar City was the principal trading port of the East African slave trade, with about 50,000 slaves a year passing through the city. The Sultan of Zanzibar controlled a substantial portion of the East African coast, known as Zanj, which included Mombasa and Dar es Salaam, and trading routes that extended much further inland, such as to Kindu on the Congo River.

Sometimes gradually, sometimes by fits and starts, control came into the hands of the British Empire; part of the political impetus for this was the 19th-century movement for the abolition of the slave trade. The relationship between Britain and the nearest relevant colonial power, Germany, was formalized by the 1890 Helgoland-Zanzibar Treaty, in which Germany pledged not to interfere with British interests in insular Zanzibar.

That year, Zanzibar became a protectorate (not a colony) of Britain. From 1890 to 1913, traditional viziers were appointed to govern as puppets, switching to a system of British residents (effectively governors) from 1913 to 1963. The death of one sultan and the succession of another, of whom the British did not approve, led to the Anglo-Zanzibar War. On the morning of 27 August 1896, the Royal Navy ships destroyed the Beit al Hukum Palace; a cease-fire was declared 38 minutes later, and the bombardment subsequently became known as The Shortest War in History.

The islands gained independence from Britain in December 1963 as a constitutional monarchy. A month later, the bloody Zanzibar Revolution, in which thousands of Arabs and Indians were killed in the genocide and thousands more expelled, established the Republic of Zanzibar and Pemba.

That April, the republic merged with the former mainland colony of Tanganyika, or more accurately, was subsumed by the much larger entity. This United Republic of Tanganyika and Zanzibar was soon renamed as a portmanteau, the United Republic of Tanzania, of which Zanzibar remains a semi-autonomous region.

CRUSADES IN ZANZIBAR.

In the early 90s, I felt a stirring in my heart for the great people of Zanzibar, so we planned and organized a crusade, knowing the resistance from some of the Muslims would be difficult. Many great Muslims might receive Christ but pay a very high price.

I sent my team with the two 18-wheelers and the team car to Dar Es Salaam to catch the cargo ferry to Zanzibar. As they arrived at Dar Es Salaam, the ship was delayed, and they had to wait a couple of days. One day, as I was praying, the Holy Spirit told me to cancel the trip to Zanzibar. As I was arguing with the Holy Spirit, I said, Lord, I don't understand. Most of the people in Zanzibar are Muslims, and they need the Gospel. Why cancel? The Lord didn't give me any explanation at all, and the Holy Spirit prompted me to obey.

I called my team leader and told him not to go with the cargo ship to Zanzibar but to return home. He was not happy at all and argued with me. I tell you, he had all the good points, but I had to follow the leading of the Holy Spirit. I told him I was his "boss," and he had to turn around and return to base in Arusha.

The cargo ship arrived at Dar Es Salaam and was loaded with trucks, cars, goods, and people, and during the night, it traveled toward Zanzibar but never made it. That night, the cargo ship collided with another bigger ship and sank to the bottom of the Indian Ocean with everyone on board. When I got the news, I was so grateful to the Holy Spirit and for the mercy of God.

If I had not listened to the voice of the Holy Spirit, I would have lost my whole team and all the crusade equipment. Maybe I would never have been able to continue with my ministry.

Later, we went back to Zanzibar, and I got the very best ground for the crusade. We got all the permits from the authorities, and everything was set for a wonderful crusade. But the night before beginning the crusade, some people who didn't want us to preach the Good News threw four pounds of dynamite toward my crusade equipment. Our God is a great God, and when the dynamite hit the stage, the fuse broke off, and the dynamite never exploded. My guards called the police, and when they arrived at the scene, the people who threw the dynamite were gone.

The next morning, the police told me I couldn't have my crusade. I told them I had all the permissions needed, and I didn't do anything wrong, and above all, I wasn't afraid.

The police told me their job was to protect me, and even they were afraid, and therefore, all my permissions were withdrawn. It really hurt me badly because I got the very best spot of all in Zanzibar to conduct a successful crusade. Also, I invested a lot of money in the crusade, and now, I wasn't allowed to preach. Again, God is great, and he gave me the greatest platform to preach to all the Swahili-speaking people of East Africa.

All the journalists showed up, and we were on the front pages of all the newspapers. Typically, we have to pay money to announce in the papers, but we got it free of charge on the front pages this time. The mobile phone rang, and it was from BBC London UK. They gave me ten minutes on live radio, broadcasting on primetime news, speaking live and direct to all East Africa. I would never have been able to use BBC London UK if it weren't for some people trying to destroy my crusade equipment. The devil is really dumb and stupid.

The Anglican Church priest invited me to use his church, which is a historic building built on top of chambers where slaves were kept before they were sold on the slave market, and there, we could conduct an indoor campaign.

It became a big story and ended up in the Tanzanian Parliament, and I got an official letter asking me to go back to Zanzibar to preach the Gospel, which I now have done several times.

During one of my crusades, I recognized a light-colored young man running forward and coming as close as possible to my stage for prayers. This young man pointed his fingers to his ears and mouth; he was deaf and mute since birth, and his parents had never heard any sound from him. I can never forget the moment when the Lord Jesus gave him his miracle and healed him completely. This young Muslim man came to my stage and had a voice for the very first time in his life but could not pronounce any words since he always had been deaf, and he had never heard a language.

I began to teach him some Swahili words, and he was able to follow me, and finally, he shouted JESUS! I had a Danish Jewish journalist video recording everything, and he made a documentary shown on Danish National TV and Norwegian National TV.

Finally, the film ended up at a film festival in San Francisco in the U.S. What the stupid and dumb devil meant to be a big failure, God turned around to be a great success.

In another Zanzibar crusade, we had a tropical rain downpour. I was hiding under a canvas and wondered why all the Muslim people didn't leave the crusade ground. I realized they wouldn't go home before I had preached and prayed for them all. I had to leave my hiding place underneath the canvas and preach in the rain. As I was preaching, I got soaking wet to my skin, and then I recognized my tie was getting shorter and shorter; it was shrinking.

I finished my preaching and gave an altar call and was surprised to see many Muslims running to the front of my stage. The whole area in front of my stage was water and mud, but nobody cared. As I began praying, the Holy Spirit came, sweeping with great power over the crowd, who by now, many of them were slain and rolling in the water and mud.

In that messy water and mud, a handicapped, paralyzed, crippled, and twisted body of a young Muslim man was healed. It was a physical transformation happening in a moment. Some people were amazed, others in awe, and others celebrated, but some were very angry, and they told this young man and his parents that they would kill him if he entered my stage to testify to his miracle.

Many of the Muslims who got saved were cut off from their families, and several precious people just disappeared.

Chapter Eighteen

THE ACADEMY OF LEADERSHIP

By Professor Oyvind Garder Anderson

I am standing on a stage in one of the towns in Tanzania, looking at the huge crowd in front of me. Dr. Egon Falk has just finished preaching, and he invites people to come forward for prayer. They come streaming, men and women, young and old, squeezing together in front of the stage.

Professor Oyvind Garder Anderson

As Dr. Egon is praying for them, they join him in prayer. Some are lifting their hands; some are weeping, some are praying at the top of their voice. They are crying out to God for the miracle they need. The atmosphere is dense. I feel surrounded by a presence of love and power; it is the presence of the Holy Spirit.

Many repent, receiving Christ as their Lord and Savior. The counselors are busy talking to them, getting their names and addresses to follow up with them. Others are touched by God's healing power. A long line is formed of people coming to the stage to testify about the healing miracles they have experienced. The crowd is rejoicing and cheering as the testimonies are told.

This is the highlight of a three-hour-long meeting. In the first part, before the preaching, there is a lot of singing and dancing. I remember how fascinated I was when I took part in the first crusade—such joy in the Lord, such enthusiasm! Different choirs, representing various churches, were singing and dancing.

These evangelistic meetings, called crusades, are prepared well in advance through Dr. Egon's and his wife Hannah's missionary organization, New Life Outreach (NLO). Churches from different denominations are brought together for the evangelistic campaign. Dr. Egon and Hannah know the Tanzanian culture well. You realize this when Dr. Egon preaches, as he does fluently in their language, Swahili. He understands how to communicate with people. The response to his jokes illustrates this.

Crusade meetings such as these have been held by Dr. Egon and Hannah for some decades now in different parts of Tanzania. I have had the privilege of taking part in several of them.

I met Hannah and Dr. Egon for the first time in the 1990s in Norway. At that time, I was a Bible school teacher belonging to the Pentecostal Movement in Norway. I had invited Hannah and Dr. Egon to tell about their missionary work in Tanzania. What they shared made a deep impression on me.

Therefore, I decided to go myself to see how these large outdoor crusade meetings worked. The first time was in 1999. I joined a crusade in Masasi, in the south of Tanzania. Dr. Egon and Hannah were already there, so I had to go by a small missionary plane, landing on a strip of grass at the outskirts of the city. Dr. Egon and Hannah had come to the airport to welcome me, making me feel at home. It was my very first trip to Africa.

The following year, in 2000, I went with a group of students to Zanzibar to take part in a crusade there. Zanzibar is an island outside of Tanzania, in union with Tanzania. While I joined Egon in teaching seminars for leaders in the mornings, the students went to villages to evangelize. In the evenings, they took part in the crusade meetings, being deeply impacted by the movement of God. A young man, for example, totally deaf in both ears, received his hearing during prayer. Probably none of the students had seen such a miracle before. People's lives can be changed forever by seeing God's power at work in such ways.

For some years, I brought even larger groups of students to Dr. Egon's crusades. I knew they would experience the work of the Holy Spirit in new and significant ways. I remember, for example, two young female students. They felt that they should spend time praying for a Tanzanian lady sitting on the ground in the crusade area. This woman was blind. But as they prayed for her, her eyes began to see. They met her the next day, and she told how she now could see the furniture in her house, the table and the chairs, and so on. The students were overwhelmed and deeply touched, realizing that God could use them in such a manner.

THE ACADEMY OF LEADERSHIP.

To win Tanzania for Christ, it is vital to train the churches' leaders—pastors, evangelists, and other leaders. Therefore, Dr. Egon and Hannah made the strategic decision to start a Bible school for leaders, the Academy of Leadership, at the NLO center in Arusha.

I have had the privilege of teaching in this school annually, for a week, from its very beginning in 2003. Thus, I have been able to follow the school's development since then. It is a biblical truth that what God does often has a small beginning. This is the story of this Bible school too. The first year, a small group of students gathered for lessons in a room that previously had been used as an office. Today, the same room is a bedroom for guests at the NLO center.

But the number of students has grown. Different facilities have been used as classrooms to accommodate the number of students. For several years, the balcony of NLO's large conference hall was used for the lectures. Some years ago, however, the Bible School got its own building with its own auditorium.

Most of the students are sponsored since they are not able to pay for the school themselves. They are pastors and leaders on different levels, but many of them have minimal educational background. Thus, such a school year is all the more needed for them. Theological training is of vital importance to ensure good and biblical preaching and teaching in the churches. But character building is also paramount. They live in a culture where corruption and other ethical issues are significant problems. Therefore, Christian leaders need to grow spiritually to be firmly rooted in Christ in all respects.

The principal, Paul Troquille, and his assistant and teacher, Reggie Moffett, are very aware of this need. Spiritual growth and character building are strongly emphasized in their training of the students.

Teaching in the school, my subject has been the gifts of the Holy Spirit. The students are so spiritually hungry. Therefore, I see a great need to teach on the work of the Spirit, to encourage the students to let themselves be used by Him—and at the same time to avoid unwise and unhealthy practices. Boldness, as well as wisdom and humility, are needed. But the spiritual hunger of the students represents a great potential for the kingdom of God.

This potential must be released, however. Therefore, not only teaching but also practice is important. In the spiritual climate of such a Bible school, I am encouraged to step out in faith myself. Therefore, at the beginning of the teaching week, I have prayed collectively for healing, sensing a great need for this among the students. This has been followed up by more individual prayer. And I have been surprised by the number of healings the students have testified about.

The leaders must be theologically and intellectually equipped for the spiritual battle and - they must be filled with the Holy Spirit and learn to act in His power.

The purpose of the Bible school is to train these pastors and leaders for the spiritual warfare going on in the country. There is a lot of witchcraft and demonic practices among the people. And there is a spiritual battle between Islam and the Christian Faith. The leaders need to be theologically and intellectually trained for this battle, and even more critical—they need to be filled with the Holy Spirit and learn to move in His power. Nothing convinces the Muslims more than seeing the miracles of God.

Presently, I am an associate professor at the Norwegian School of Leadership and Theology in Oslo in Norway. This school has a twofold vision: theological training on an academic level and ministering in the power of the Holy Spirit. Therefore, it is very good for me to take part in the work of New Life Outreach, thereby getting opportunities to be in the mission field myself, experiencing the work of the Spirit. Coming back to Norway, I can share my experiences with people there, encouraging them in their faith. Thus, what God does in Tanzania can also be a blessing for Norway.

I have already mentioned the principal, Paul Troquille, and his assistant and teacher, Reggie Moffett. Reggie's wife, Ronnan, is also a part of the team, as well as Paul's wife, Debbie. It is always a blessing to be with them at the NLO center, fellowshipping with them and getting to share in their vision for the students and the school. Their purpose-focused way of living and their prioritizing of what counts for eternity inspires and challenges me. And they take such good care of me and my wife, Yvonne, when we stay there, making us feel at home.

Nkongi, a Tanzanian man, has been my interpreter since the start of the school. It is such a blessing to work with him. He is trustworthy and is doing excellent work as an interpreter.

EXAMPLES OF NETWORKING.

Taking part in NLO's work has made it possible for me to connect with other ministers in Tanzania to join in the battle for the kingdom of God. Let me give some examples, which also illustrate the spiritual condition in Tanzania.

Dickson Kaganga is the pastor of an Assemblies of God church in Zanzibar. About 98% of the inhabitants of Zanzibar are Muslims. In the year 2000, I preached in his church during Egon's crusade. They were about 80 people gathered under a simple roof of bamboo branches, but I was struck by the strong presence of God in this church. Five years later, I came back. The church had then grown to about 500, and they had a large church building. Later, it had doubled and has several daughter churches as well.

The growth of Dickson's church illustrates the spiritual battle going on in the country. Some years ago, a large mob of Muslims attacked the church while Dickson was in the office preparing the Sunday service. They destroyed a part of the wall surrounding the church, set the main door on fire, gathered the plastic chairs in the church hall as well, and set them on fire too. It is a miracle that the thin curtain covering the wall behind the stage did not catch fire because behind this curtain, there was a door to Dickson's office, where he was sitting. If it had been found, he would probably have been killed. He was, however, able to call the police, and the attackers ran away. I visited the church and saw the damaged building. Later, Dr. Egon had a crusade in Dickson's rebuilt church.

Another example is Wilson Gwimo, the late bishop for The Free Pentecostal Churches of Tanzania (FPCT) in the Kigoma region, at the lake of Tanganyika. (FPCT is a fruit of Swedish Pentecostal missionary work.) They have many members in this area. Wilson was, as a bishop, a student at the Academy of Leadership in one of the first years of the school. Talking to him during my week of teaching, we agreed to arrange a crusade together in Kigoma. We did so in 2009.

In a seminar in his church, ahead of the crusade meetings outdoors, a woman came for prayer for pain in her head. As I looked at her, I saw that one of her eyes seemed totally dead. You could only see the white color of the eye, no pupil or iris—or perhaps one millimeter of the iris in the corner of that eye. I asked myself: is there any purpose in praying for this? I began, however, to pray for the pain. As I was doing so, suddenly, she said that she could see my hand with that blind eye. The pupil came forward, but it did not coordinate well with the other eye at first. As we continued to pray, however, the two eyes coordinated perfectly. It was awesome to see this happen before my eyes. Miracles such as this are what we need as signs following the preaching of the Gospel.

Hannah and Egon Falk made the strategic decision to start a Bible school for leaders, The Academy of Leadership, at the NLO Center in Arusha.

THE VISION OF DR. EGON AND HANNAH FALK.

The kingdom of God has, in many ways, had significant breakthroughs in the nation of Tanzania. Yet, the country is still marked by much spiritual darkness. It is Egon and Hannah's vision to let the light of the Gospel penetrate this darkness.

Dr. Egon and Hannah know well that more than preaching is needed to accomplish this task. The Gospel must be preached in the power of the Holy Spirit, with signs and wonders, to see people brought from darkness to light, from the bondage of Satan to the kingdom of God. The apostle Paul expressed the importance of this in his letter to the Romans, stating that he ministered by "the power of signs and miracles, through the power of the Spirit" (Rom 15:19). This is what characterizes the ministry of Dr. Egon and Hannah too. The powerful healings and miracles that happen in their meetings are vital to the harvest they see in terms of thousands of people receiving salvation through faith in Christ.

Dr. Egon and Hannah are the kind of people that really inspire and challenge me. They have devoted their lives to bringing people to Christ ever since they first came to Tanzania as missionaries. Even though they could have retired because of their age, they are still pressing on to see more of the spiritual darkness dispelled, to see more people saved for eternity. They have not lost their focus but demonstrate what it means to do the work of Him who sent us, while it is day, before the night is coming, when no one can work (John 9:4).

It is a blessing to work with Dr. Egon and Hannah to join them in preaching the Gospel and training leaders who can carry on the work and multiply it. Also, fellowshipping with them in their home in Arusha has been a great joy for Yvonne and me.

Chapter Nineteen
SMALL BEGINNINGS

There was a time I didn't have a car to drive me to the different places doing ministry to people, so I had to use public transportation. One time, I was riding the public bus. It was a very old bus, and the seat was just an iron bar, and my window couldn't close one bit.

When the night and darkness arrived, we suddenly hit a nasty pothole, and all the lights went off, and it became pitch-dark. The driver couldn't continue driving without the lights. It was up in the mountains and very cold; it was the longest night I've ever experienced in my life.

Another time, I was preaching in a small village without any hotels or guesthouses, so I stayed in the pastor's hut along with hundreds of rats. There was no electricity, only a locally made oil lamp, and when I blew it out, it became pitch dark.

When the pastor realized that I had blown out the oil lamp during the night, he told me not to do that. Why? If the light were on all night, I wouldn't have any rats in my bed because they don't like the light, just like the demons from hell.

No running water in the bathroom. Did I say bathroom? It was just a surrounding made from dry grass, and everyone in the village was watching me taking my "shower" out of a small bucket. When I went to the "bathroom," every child shouted, "White man is taking a shower."

After one week, leaving this village was somehow a joy, but the bus was late, and I was sitting under a tree waiting for six hours. Finally, the bus arrived, but the front windshield wasn't there anymore. No problem—we got our air-conditioning along with a lot of dust.

We made it to the main road, expecting to catch another bus to our final destination for another Gospel outreach.

But there was no bus because I was late, and it was a dark evening. Finally, I got a lift with a truck packed with a lot of

people. I was the only white man, and everyone looked strangely at me.

At midnight, I arrived at my destination and was welcomed by three or four people, the only Christians in that village. I got a small room in their home and just dropped "dead" on the bed and slept until the next morning.

I had the first Gospel outreach in that village preaching at the market, standing on a stool, shouting the Good News to the hundreds of listeners without a loudspeaker. I tell you, when a white man is standing on a stool shouting, you will have a crowd. This was the beginning of a breakthrough and a church with hundreds of Christians today.

MY BIGGEST MONEY MIRACLE OF $305,000.

No missionaries can work and minister without money, and very often, missionaries live and work under very poor conditions.

Needs on the mission field are so many and enormous, and it's painful to see the suffering among the local people.

It is so easy to get distracted by the many needs and all the suffering, but nobody can help everyone.

You have to love all the people and help as many you can—show the love of Jesus, but at the same time, you need to focus on what God called you to do.

God called me to preach the Gospel of Jesus, bringing hope and change for those who receive Christ.

In the footsteps of preaching the Gospel, God led us to start New Life Schools with a capacity of 1,000 children and youth. Hayley's House is a home connected to New Life Schools, which is for orphans and girls with special needs.

In connection with the campaigns, a textbook by John Bevere will also be distributed to priests and evangelists.

Since I don't have the calling and gift of pastoring, I never planned to plant a church in Arusha. But in the footsteps of the Gospel, we planted New Life City Church, which is a blessing to so many people, and within a few years, there will be many New Life City Churches all over Tanzania.

Also, in the footsteps of the Gospel, we began to teach pastors, evangelists, and ministers. Birthed out of our Academy of Leadership Bible Colleges in Arusha, Tanzania, we now have 46 Satellite Bible Schools all over the country.

From the festive graduation party for the trained leaders.

As our Academy of Leadership Bible College expanded, we needed a bigger building. After I legally bought a piece of land and began the building program, we ran into so many problems and ended up in a court case. Finally, we won the case, but I didn't have any more money, only debt. I was confused and repeatedly asked the Lord why no money came for this very important building program. God didn't give me any answers at all, and we couldn't move on and get into even more debt.

Sometimes, it seems that God is late, but I have learned that He isn't.

At the Fire for The Nations Conference at Pastors Mark and Janet Brazee's World Outreach Church in Tulsa, Oklahoma, USA, on a Monday night, our dear friend and Pastor Sam Carr was led by the Holy Spirit to take up an offering for our building program. Our need was $225,000 just for the building itself. It's very difficult to explain what happened that night. The movement of God was so strong and wonderful, and in just a few minutes, we had $250,000, and before the money was wired to our bank in Tanzania, the amount was $305.000.

We have expanded again and again and needed more equipment, cars, trucks, and buildings, and you know it costs money, big money indeed—but miracles happen again and again.

It seems that God never allows us to stay in our comfort zone when it comes to money. He wants us to be totally dependent on and trusting Him and Him alone.

GIVING LOVE, HOPE, CHANGE, AND FUTURE TO THE LOST AND HURTING PEOPLE.

Jesus had and still has love and passion for the lost and hurting people, and so should we.

As Christian followers of Jesus, we don't live for ourselves anymore, and if we live for Jesus, we also live for the people of this world as He did during His time on earth.

Selfishness has a very ugly face, but Christ Jesus's face reflects the giving love of God, and so should we.

I can't ever forget the day I first saw this skinny little 10-year-old Masai girl called Helena. Her eyes were dead, no light at all. Depression was written all over her—no hope and no future.

Helena's mother had died, and her father sold her to be the wife of a Masai warrior with four wives. Only ten years old and bound to "slavery." What a pain!

We took Helena into our Hayley's House, a home for girls with special needs—surely, Helena qualified.

We prayed with Helena and loved on her, and now, after 15 years, she is a beautiful, well-educated Christian young lady.

Neema was just a baby when her dad was murdered. Her mother had a very difficult time just surviving and lived from day to day.

One evening, Neema was sitting in her mother's lap when some bandits forcefully entered the little room, and with a big machete, cleaved off her mother's head.

When Neema came to us, she was in very bad shape, but through love and care, she is now a wonderful young lady with a great future ahead of her.

Sometimes, we are overwhelmed and tired, but we should never forget to show the love and passion of Jesus to hurting people without any hope in this world.

WE HAVE LEFT EVERYTHING TO FOLLOW YOU, JESUS!

In the Gospel of Mark 10:28, Peter said to Jesus, "We have left everything to follow you!"

Sometimes, I feel the same way. I left my family, friends, church, job, and nation. I missed out on many family and friends' weddings, celebrations, Christmas, Easter, birthdays, and even funerals, and the list goes on and on.

I had to send my children to a boarding school far away from their home in Tanzania to Kenya, a neighboring nation,

which I didn't want to do, but I had to give my children the best possible school education. It was painful for my children and even us as parents. I felt I failed in my responsibility as a loving dad.

My family and I missed the luxury life, which people in the Western world take for granted.

My family lived through times with no money and an empty refrigerator. No soda pop, no ice-cream, nor any kind of snacks.

No TV, no iPad and computer games, nor any cinema movie visit with popcorn and Coke. The NO list is endless.

Even when the refrigerator was empty, my wife Hannah managed to create the most delicious dinners for us as a family and even more for the many guests we always have in our house. Here is a testimony from a dear friend. "Dear Egon and, of course, Hannah, Happy Birthday, Hannah! I will

bless your wife like this, Egon! Every time I hear of your ministry, I am reminded of my friend Herbert Fischer, who used to work for and maybe still is with CFAN. He told me that one of the highlights of doing ministry with Reinhard Bonnke was when they had the chance to stay with you guys in Arusha. He told me about your hospitality and about the delicious food you provided for them.

So, my blessing to your wife is this: Rumors about her hospitality have reached as far as Norway, and they make me think—wish I was there... You are both blessed."

I know my dear wife and children "suffered" silently because they all wanted their dad to serve and preach the Gospel to the whole nation of Tanzania, for which I am forever grateful, and I feel I am in debt to them. Without my wife and children's support, I would never be able to live out God's calling for my life.

"I tell you the truth," Jesus replied, "no one who has left home or brothers or sisters or mother or father or children or fields for me and the gospel will fail to receive a hundred times as much in this present age (homes, brothers, sisters, mothers, fathers, children and fields—and with them persecutions) and in the age to come, eternal life."

> *I NEVER REGRET FOLLOWING CHRIST AND GOD'S CALLING UPON MY LIFE. GOD IS A GOOD GOD—PERIOD!*

THE FUTURE.

It's funny; now that I am 72 years old, people ask me when I will stop my ministry for the Lord and the people. Yes, I know I am getting older, but I will never stop my ministry!!! How can you stop living? My ministry is my life, and if I stop, I will die.

I am in transition, handing some work areas over to the younger generation, which every founder and leader should do. Still, I will continue and focus on preaching the Gospel through my big crusades and teaching the Word of God.

I am also a spiritual father to so many spiritual children, who now are serving God, and I will never abandon them.

I will continue working in Africa, Jordan, and Myanmar, and other places as the Holy Spirit will lead me.

With my lifelong experience, I believe I still can do a lot for the Kingdom of God, and I believe the best is yet to come. I want to prove the people wrong who believe an old man can't serve God, and I challenge you to support me financially, and you will be blessed more than ever before!

GREAT MEN OF GOD.

During the years of ministry, I have met many wonderful people from all over the world who have supported and encouraged me a lot, and it's impossible to mention them all in this book, but I want to mention a few.

Reinhard Bonnke was a great inspiration for me, and I will never forget an evening we had together in my house during his Crusade in Arusha, Tanzania.

Aril Edvardsen has been a wonderful friend to me since I was very young. I am so thankful for his generous support and the many crusades and pastors' seminars we did together in Tanzania.

Pastors Jan Halvorsen, Gunnar Jeppestøl, Geir Stomnås, David Hansen, Knud Ipsen, Frede Rasmussen, Frank Bailey, Randy Cilluffo, Rusty Martin, Mark Brazee, Paul Troquille, Paulo Samwel, and many more have impacted my life and ministry significantly.

For that, I am thankful, but there is one man of God who has impacted me the most and also become my very best friend. It's Pastor Sam Carr from Life United in Shreveport, LA, USA. When God connected Pastor Sam and me, my ministry rapidly began to grow tremendously.

I am eternally thankful for every man of God and all the churches who made my ministry flourish and bring millions of precious people into the Kingdom of God.

I am also very thankful to the Board of New Life Outreach in Denmark and Tanzania.

It would be wrong if I didn't mention my godly, sweet, wonderful wife, Hannah, my children Tina, Ruben, and Gitte, and the whole family, plus... **TOGETHER, WE MADE IT HAPPEN!**

Chapter Twenty
A CHILD OF A MISSIONARY
By Tina Falk, Hannah & Egon's firstborn child

Hey Daddy,

If you should have forgotten, I want to remind you that you have been a super fantastic dad from day one.

You have been a dad who NEVER left your children and who NEVER betrayed your children.

You have been a dad who taught your children some incredible values.

We learned from you to work hard.

We learned from you to be dutiful.

We learned from you to love with a big heart.

Tina Falk, Hannah & Egon's firstborn child

We learned from you that it's honorable to be able to say, "forgive me."

We learned from you that it's a blessing to forgive.

We learned from you to fight like a lion for what we love.

We learned from you that justice is something the stronger ones have to fight for on behalf of the weaker ones.

We have learned from you that marriage and family are a precious jewel, a gift from God.

We have learned from you who the only true almighty wonderful God is.

We have learned from you who Jesus is.

We have also learned from you to live life, have fun, and enjoy life as the gift it is.

I could continue to remind you all you have taught us three children, but then it would become a whole book.

You are the best dad in the whole world.

Since I was a little girl, I have adored you and admired you so much.

You have always been my hero, and I love you!

Egon and Hannah with their 3 children Tina, Ruben and Gitte on their parents' 45th wedding anniversary.

It was a summer day in Denmark in the year 2020, and I was sitting on the train going back to my hometown, Hillerød, after spending some lovely time with my dear parents in my sister's vacation home.

During dinner time the evening before, we had, as many

times before, talked about our lives and the ups and downs of living a life of service in the mission field and ministry.

I was talking about the pain and impact my parents' ministry has had on my childhood and life, and I said, "Dad, I feel that I have no voice in all of this."

My dad surprised me with his response; he invited me to write a little passage for this book on how I have experienced being a missionary daughter.

Riding on the train going back home, I looked out onto the beautiful Danish fields, seeing Danish farmhouses, fields of yellow flowers, and fields of red flowers passing me by.

As I looked at the typical Danish cows and saw deer and a couple of ginger red foxes running to safety behind trees and bushes, I thought that my mum and dad are very brave to invite me to talk openly about how I have experienced being a missionary daughter.

I was full of excitement and eager to start writing.

A couple of months later, I still had not written anything because it filled me with emotional pain and sadness.

I was so conflicted in my thoughts.

How can I write without hurting my parents or without sounding bitter?

I love and adore my parents, and I love and support their mission work, and I love Tanzania.

I love and honor God, and my heart and whole life belong to Jesus Christ, my Savior, and Lord.

As I am writing this, I am a 50- year-old lady, and I am the proud mother of three lovely grown children.

Most of my childhood and upbringing was spent in Tanzania and Kenya, attending English boarding schools.

I was growing up as my parents' ministry was being born and setting off.

I loved growing up in beautiful Africa, and I always thought that I would serve alongside my parents in New Life Outreach.

But it didn't quite turn out like that.

As far back as I remember, my parents have actively been in ministry, serving God.

I was born into a life of ministry and service.

As my parents matured and their ministry grew, they gave their whole lives to serving God.

Their time and focus seemed only to be on God and their calling and ministry.

As I was growing up, I found it increasingly difficult to get and maintain my parents' attention.

I found it difficult to attend boarding school, and I missed my parents so much.

When you grow up in boarding school, you don't have the opportunity to come home at the end of the day.

No mom or dad tucks you in at bedtime for the night, and if you have experienced difficulties during your school day with your peers or with school, there are no loving, embracing parents that can comfort, help, or protect you.

I had several different boarding parents in various boarding houses during my school life.

I can't remember their names or faces because they were never very close or involved with their boarding children.

The doors between the boarding kids' house and the dorm parents were always closed.

When the dorm parents entered the dorm, their attention was mostly on the English and American kids.

The kids that came from non-English speaking countries often did not receive as much attention as the English-speaking kids and they did not focus on the children that were having difficulties.

One evening, as I crawled into bed, I was extremely sad and homesick.

I was sharing a bedroom with three other girls.

That day, the other girls excluded me from their social activity, and I was left out.

I could hear all the other girls gathering in the other bedroom, deciding to have "a sleepover."

I was not part of the fun they had together, and as I laid down trying to go to sleep, I felt so homesick.

I sobbed as I tried to read my Bible.

It was a warm African night; there was no wind blowing in the trees or bushes outside, and the windows were closed.

I could hear the girls next door laughing, the watchmen talking softly outside, and a dog barking in the distance.

I was overwhelmed with sadness.

Suddenly, I felt the presence of someone entering the room, but I couldn't see anyone.

I felt the presence sitting down on my bed.

I could see and feel the impression of someone sitting on my bed.

I didn't feel fear; I knew at once it was the Holy Spirit.

There was a very soft wind blowing over me, and I felt the wind stroking my tear-filled face, and without verbal voice, the presence of the Holy Spirit spoke to me words of soothing comfort just as if I had my mum or dad sitting there.

I experienced many things during my childhood.

I have faced lions, snakes, and malaria, among other things.

Once, we were a group of school children sitting on an open truck out on a school trip.

The truck broke down, and lions gathered around us, getting ready to jump up on the truck and attack.

We were sitting ducks, and we understood the danger.

I started praying to God, and suddenly out of nowhere, a young antelope jumped out of a small bush and ran between the truck and the lions.

God saved us.

Tina and Ruben with African friends on Sanjaranda in 1974 just after the family's arrival in Tanzania.

I have had malaria many times. For one incident, I was at home in Arusha with my parents and siblings.

I woke up one Sunday morning, and I could feel at once that I was sick with malaria again.

I choose to go with my family to the Sunday service.

I was about 16 years old, and as my father preached and got ready to pray for the sick, I raised my hands and asked God to heal me.

At once, I felt the presence of the Holy Spirit flow through me, and I felt strong and healthy again.

That was the last time I had malaria for the rest of my time in Africa.

One thing I found extremely difficult to deal with through my upbringing and many times in my adult life is that I have to share my parents with the rest of the world.

When I came home for a vacation stay from boarding school in my childhood home in Arusha, our family home was the base for the mission, and the house was increasingly filled with volunteers from Scandinavia, and everybody was busy working for the ministry.

It was difficult getting time alone with my parents.

As I got older, I felt my emotional pain and sadness growing deeper.

I struggled with emotional hurt in my teens, and I longed for and needed my parents' attention and love.

I felt my parents couldn't understand me, and I felt that they didn't have the time and patience that were needed.

I grew up sensing and feeling that I was too needy and difficult, and with the sentence hanging over my head, there is always someone out there that is suffering more than me.

So, I also felt very guilty for having so much emotional pain and sadness.

Sometimes, I could only be alone with my parents in their bedroom.

On one occasion, the house was alive with activity and people.

My parents were in their bedroom.

Dad was sitting at his desk, working on his sermon; Mom was handling the clean laundry.

I sat on their bed and tried to talk to them about my struggles.

My dad started to turn around to face me.

I felt a small feeling of hope growing inside me. I had their full attention; the door for communication opened, and I felt that now we could talk. Suddenly, a volunteer walked in and demanded my parents' help and attention.

Years later, after I had moved back to Denmark as a 19-year-old girl, I struggled to feel at home as a Dane in a country that felt strange and foreign to me.

I really didn't know anyone, and I had no close relations with any family members such as uncles, aunts, or grandparents due to my upbringing in Africa.

I was sent to Denmark alone without my parents' support because their ministry demanded their time and attention.

I felt so alone and abandoned, and it was a great culture shock for me.

It took me seven long years before I could feel at home in my own country.

As a child, young girl, and young woman, I have needed my mother on many occasions, but my mother has mostly been far away, side by side with my father, serving God faithfully.

Mostly when my parents visit Denmark, we can have one day together.

I don't have them close enough to be able to just pop by for a visit. When the kids were young, there were no grandparents to visit or babysit the kids.

The ministry, crusades, leading multitudes to Christ, praying for the sick, and deliverance for people in need always has and will always be far more important than my children and me. I support this because I know this calling and ministry is the will of God.

When I was a young teenager, I understood this, and I gave my parents to God.

I was struck in my heart with a deep love for Africa and deep love for people to meet Jesus Christ, so I said to God, you can have my parents; I give them to you.

For years, I struggled to find my own place in ministry.

I had a deep desire to serve God and serve God alongside my parents, but I felt there was no place for me.

I could write much more but will end with saying that there have been many fun, loving, and exciting experiences and blessings growing up as a missionary daughter, but there has been and still is also a price to pay.

Though I believe that the blessing far succeeds the lack, hurt, and pain.

As I was riding home on the train that summer day in the

year 2020, I said again to God, with love in my heart and tears in my eyes, You can have my parents; I give them to you.

As a young woman, the Holy Spirit led me to Psalm 27 verse 10, and I have often returned to that scripture.

God is always faithful and true to his promise.

Chapter Twenty-One
A MISSIONARY CHILD'S SCHOOL TALE
By Ruben Falk, son of Hannah & Egon Falk

Dear Dad,

Today is your birthday, and you are 72 years old. Of course, you are out preaching today in Haderslev, Denmark. This is your life's passion: to share God's love with people.

You, Mom, and I have accomplished a lot together; it's not small.

Ruben Falk, son of Hannah & Egon Falk

I love you. You are a true role model in life and service, and I admire your pioneer spirit.

There are both good and difficult sides to growing up as a missionary child. My upbringing as one has not been much different from other missionary children.

A missionary child encounters a broad palette of emotions and feelings that define who they are as third-culture kids. Third-culture child is a term used to describe children who grow up abroad in different cultures than their own. Often, they move around quite a bit during their childhood and attend boarding schools or international schools where they meet other children with a background much like their own or come from affluent families in the local community.

First, there is the excitement of leaving your home country, school, church, and friends and traveling to a foreign land. I remember my sisters and I being very excited about this and seeing it as an exciting adventure.

I do not remember much from our first trip to the mission field. I mostly remember stories told repeatedly by my parents and people that knew us back then. I was around three years old when my parents left Norway and went to Singida in Tanzania as missionaries. I only have a few glimpses and pictures in my mind of that time. These glimpses and images are romantic memories of encounters with spiders, lizards, snakes, and roaming the neighborhood with the local children. I remember learning how to use a slingshot. One of the more vivid memories I have is hitting my cheek on the edge of a table and how we had to rush on a long drive to a Catholic mission hospital, where my cheek could be sewed with a couple of stitches. I also remember our vacation times at the beaches south of Mombasa in Kenya, where we would play in the waves all day long.

My dad would go out into the bush to small villages on Sundays to preach, and he brought us along into small dark, dusty churches. After church, we were often invited into the homes of the local pastors for lunch. The homes were constructed by building a small structure of wooden branches and covering these branches with dung and mud.

The floors inside the houses were made of hardened mud. Furniture in the houses was scarce and often just consisted of small stools to sit on. The food prepared for us consisted of ugali (a thickened maize porridge), beans, rice, and spinach. If we were lucky, we would also have a variety of soupy sauce with chunks of chicken or goat meat. The food was poured onto large plates for sharing, each person taking the food directly in front of them. The food quality would vary, and it was always with some risk of stomachache and running bowels that you would partake in the meal.

On our first trip to the mission field is where I have my first memory of chili sauce. My dad has always been fond of ketchup, and on one trip to Arusha, we had fries at a restaurant, and my dad saw the bottle of ketchup on the table and lavished it over his fries. There was only one problem with that; it was not ketchup but chili sauce. I remember laughing so hard that my stomach hurt.

Back then, we did not know much about chili sauce.

My mom was pregnant on this first missionary trip, and my little sister came into the world at the same mission hospital where I got my stitches. My older sister and I never considered what gender the baby would have, but we had long talks about what color skin our sibling would have when she came into the world—would it be black or white? We really did not know.

After three years in the dusty and windy town Singida, we moved back to Denmark to a town called Esbjerg. This is where I have my first real memories. Even though my parents are Danish and I am a Dane, I was not born in Denmark but in Norway. When I was born, my dad was a traveling evangelist in Norway, and we lived there. Back to Esbjerg—as we moved to the town, I was about six or seven years old. I did not speak much Danish but conversed in a mixture of Norwegian and Kiswahili. At this age, I also started school. Thinking back to starting school fills me with many mixed emotions. The reason for this is that this is where it dawned upon me that I was different from everybody else.

I had not grown up in a regular suburb with Mom and Dad going off to work every day. I did not have the same Danish cultural memories as the other kids. When they told stories of riding bikes, I would be telling stories about killing snakes, lizards, or birds and seeing lions and elephants in the wild. I did not speak Danish like the other children but conversed in a mixture of Norwegian and Kiswahili. Furthermore, my dad was not a mason or carpenter but a pastor and preacher. This led to a lot of curiosity from the other children in school, and unfortunately, it also led to being teased and conflicts with some children because of my story. I did not really feel that the teachers at the school supported or understood me. The school left me exposed as different and left me with a sense of not belonging. Even though school sucked, Esbjerg was not bad. I had good friends that I would roam the neighborhood with. At the end of six years in Esbjerg, my parents announced that we were moving back to Tanzania again, this time to Dar es Salaam. Being adventurous, I thought this was cool and really looked forward to it.

Back in Tanzania, we spent a couple of months in a guesthouse in Dar es Salaam while my parents looked for a house that we could rent. Evidently, this was difficult. When my dad was offered a position as a manager with the Christian Radio station —Radio Habari Maluum in Arusha, we moved to Arusha, where we settled down as a family. While at the guest house in Dar es Salaam, Mom homeschooled us, and I learned the multiplication tables really well—actually like our lives depended on it.

In Arusha, I was enrolled at a local English-speaking school called St. Constantin International School. Again, language was an issue. During the six years in Denmark, I had learned to speak and write Danish, and in that process, I had forgotten to speak Norwegian and Kiswahili. So, upstart at the "Greek" School, as we called the school, was rough, but English came pretty fast. I experienced one episode where I was called to the front of the class to do something on the blackboard. I tried to find the English word for "sand" in my memory, but only came up with the Norwegian word for shower "dush." It left both me, the teacher, and the other students frustrated and confused.

At the Greek School, I did get the feeling of belonging because I met up with kids from many different nations and cultures. At the school, there were Europeans, Asians, Indians, Tanzanians, and Americans. There was a mutual feeling of understanding that our differences were what made us alike. At this school, I had a Norwegian friend whose dad was an expatriate and worked for some Norwegian power-grid project. Coming from an atheistic background in Norway, my Norwegian friend got himself into a serious discussion in a classroom setting where he ridiculed people groups that believed in a divine entity and had religious faith. I remember most of the class considering him naive and stupid because he thought there was no God. During this episode, it dawned on me that the sense of belonging that I felt at this school was because I was together with other kids where faith was foundational. This feeling has stayed with me over the years.

After one year at the Greek School and at the age of 12, I moved away from home to a boarding school called the International School of Moshi (ISM). The school was situated in the town of Moshi in the foothills of Mount Kilimanjaro, 85 kilometers from Arusha. Therefore, my older sister and I had to board at the school and only travel home for weekends. ISM was something totally different from the Greek School. In my memories, the Greek school is remembered as a place of innocence, a good place to be. I also understand that my memories of the school most likely are romantic, and reality could have been different.

In contrast to that, ISM is where I lost my innocence and had to deal with

the realities of teenage life. Like many other teenage boys, I battled with my identity and need to belong to a group. This led me, together with my friends, to experiment with smoking, drinking, and girls. One thing that I did not experiment with, though, was marijuana and drugs. Marijuana and drugs were easily accessible around the school, but it is something that I have always been afraid of. Being an insecure young teenage boy, I was afraid of not fitting in and being cool with the rest of the boys. Therefore, when there was a party, I gave it all I had.

At the Greek school, I found a sense of belonging in that

all the other kids at the school also had faith, but at ISM, this changed. As I remember it, ISM was much more divided into ethnic and religious groups, at times, creating tensions between these groups. I remember good friendships, fun activities, trips, and good times. At ISM, I learned to play football and tennis and to ride a horse. I joined the mountain club and got to climb the mountain peaks of Longido, Meru, and Kilimanjaro. Our class geography, history, and biology field trip to Pangani, an old slave town on the cost 90 kilometers south of Tanga, has left an everlasting impression on me. Another fond memory I have from ISM is hiking up the local river that ran close to the school. The river was off-limits, and the school did not want us to roam around there. But we did; we loved to hike up the small waterfalls and swim in the cold water. We would build small shelters where we could hang out and climb up sheer cliffs, daring each other to keep going. On one of these trips to the river, we encountered a huge snake on the path. It scared us so much that we ran as fast as we could all the way back to the school and did not hike up the river for a very long time.

The four years I spent at ISM are filled with mixed memories, some I would like to be without and some that I cherish dearly. My ISM experience led me to a decision that I upheld many years later when I brought my own family onto the mission field, a decision that my kids would never attend boarding school. My kids need their mother and me during the fragile teenage years when boys become men and girls women.

Keeping us children in school was not cheap and something that my dad worked hard at through the years. He would look for new business opportunities that could keep his children in school. Back in the nineteen-eighties, we drove brand-new four-wheel vehicles and a new Mercedes Benz to school because he was flipping cars to make money to pay for our tuition. In the nineteen-eighties, Tanzania was run by politics that did not allow the locals to import anything. So, the local businessmen had so much cash lying around that they did not know what to do with it.

On the other hand, they were so desperate to purchase vehicles to drive that they would approach my dad and offer him truckloads of cash if they could purchase his vehicle. This kept us in school and secured us nice vehicles to drive. This brings me to one of the things that I most admire about my dad. He has a sense of stubbornness and faith that surpasses everything; this faith and stubbornness often make him a first mover, and he walks down paths that have not been walked earlier. I believe this is one of the major reasons he has been able to endure and build New Life Outreach. He will not give up, and he will not allow a lack of funds to determine the outcome or result. He would always seek the kingdom of God first and his will, and when he knew the will of God, my dad also knew how he would deal with it. Over

the years, he has encountered many hardships working for God in the mission field, but these days, you cannot go anywhere in Tanzania without meeting people who know who my dad is and have a story to tell about their encounter with him. My dad is a people person; even though he speaks to the masses, he always sees the individual and has time for that one person.

ISM was not my last experience with boarding school. After four years, I was moved to a boarding school by the name of Rift Valley Academy (RVA). The school is located in the village of Kijabe, 55 kilometers west of Nairobi, Kenya's capital. Because the school was in a different country than Tanzania, my sister and I could not go home on weekends but had to stay at the school for six weeks and only go home for holidays. RVA is a Christian boarding school with a vision of offering education to children of missionaries working all over Africa.

I spent two years at RVA. During this time, I met a form of discipline and correction of children and teenagers I disagree with. In my memories, I remember RVA for two things: First, if you are not good at sports or academics, then why are you here?

Either you are a troublemaker or not very bright! Second, I found a legalistic form of Christianity that based a holy relationship with God on following a set of rigid rules. Breaking these rules would lead to severe punishment and you not being a "good" Christian. As a young man, I detested this form of Christianity and longed for God's grace and mercy; a relationship with God based on the Holy Spirit being alive and living on your inside, instead of a holiness quest, based on following a set of religious rules deemed to be Godly rules by our Christian peers.

When attending non-Christian schools, you expect that the other students and teachers do not understand what it means to be a Christian or a missionary. I was shocked at RVA because here, I learned that there is the right way to be a missionary and a not-so-right way. The right way to be a missionary would be to move out into a third-world country and settle in a community where you would make a difference and show Christ through different social projects to help the poor and needy. By doing this, you could point to Christ and encourage the community to attend church. I have nothing against this type of missionary. The approach is anchored in the New Testament, and Christian communities worldwide are founded this way. But what shocked me was the attitude that the way my parents were missionaries was the not-so-right way. What was it that my parents did that was not the right way? Well, my parents have always tended to the needy and poor, but this is not where their passion is. Their passion is to preach the gospel of Jesus Christ, that there is a Heaven and Hell, that eternity is real. That Jesus has come to forgive and to save. The not-so-right missionary approach was that my parents believed in healing the sick and casting out demons, praying for people that they may experience the baptism of the Holy Spirit and speak in new tongues. This missionary approach was looked down upon by my RVA peers—both teachers and students.

At RVA, I belonged to a group of students that did not care for academics and were not great at sports. Often, I was left with the feeling that the teachers frowned on us. A big part of the junior and senior year was the annual banquet. I remember during our junior year, how we spent a lot of time building and preparing for the banquet; it was our job to set the theme. We built a whole southern theme for the party. I thought it was fun; I have always enjoyed working with my hands. I do remember detesting the whole hype about asking a girl as a banquet date. Being part of the "misfit group," we were expected to ask the less popular girls and make sure that all girls had a date. We went along with this during our junior year, but as we became seniors at the school, we decided to throw a curveball at our senior banquet. We decided to ask all the popular girls to be our dates early in the year and beat the popular boys to it.

This plan went very well, and I remember that I got a yes from one of the nicest girls at school. She did very well both in academics and sports. We thought this was very fun until a message came down from the school office, saying that all banquet agreements were canceled and we had to ask again. We did not think that this was fair and decided that we would not ask anybody as a date for the banquet. This did not sit well with the school office, and we were told to play along or we would not be allowed to attend the banquet.

RVA did have its bright moments. I did find good friends, and the junior and senior year field trips were great. I went rock climbing to Mount Kenya's summit, one of the greatest mountaineering trips in my life, and second, I went on a motorcycling safari into northern parts of Kenya. These are memories that I cherish to this day.

At the end of my two years at RVA, I had turned 18 years old, and it was time to head to Denmark for further studies.

I have talked to many people who think it must be traumatizing to grow up at different boarding schools as a child. I know that it is for some, and they battle with it for the rest of their lives. For me, boarding school was a tough life, where you must be able to take care of yourself. I am alright with the above story.

Personally, I will not send my children off to boarding school, but we all must make choices as adults and parents. These choices affect the wellbeing of others, and we must live with that for better or worse. I respect my parents' choice to send us three children off to boarding school and trust God to take care of us. What has been a harder battle for me and still is today is that some think serving God has priority over family; that is difficult for me to accept. I truly believe that God has entrusted us with family for us to love and care for, that family is the highest priority that God has entrusted to us. It precedes any ministry opportunity that we have. When I mention this, it shames me to say that I have fallen short of the family value and have prioritized ministry over family in my ministry.

My greatest dream was to become an engineer and move back out to the third-world and make a difference with my skills. This never happened because, after a couple of years in Denmark studying, God touched my life and totally transformed me. This is where I will close my trip down memory lane. Because when God touches you, a new chapter opens and being my father's son, I leaped into this chapter headfirst, not thinking too much and not calculating the costs. The chapter involves becoming a man, husband, father, and, of course, becoming a missionary, pastor, and principal and working with my parents on and off the mission field for 25 years. I can share this tale with you in the future.

Closing my contribution to this book, it is important for me to say that there are no regrets in me, but I am who I am. I am a third-culture child, rounded and shaped by my story. I will most likely always feel that I do not belong, which is alright with me today. I have come to terms with the turmoil that I, at times, can feel on my inside. What is much more important for me today is what I can contribute and how I can make a difference for less fortunate people than me.

Chapter Twenty-Two

BUSH BABY

By Gitte Falk Jakobsen, Hannah & Egon's youngest child

In many ways, growing up on the missionary field has been just as normal as any other childhood.

I had a family, siblings to play and argue with, cats and dogs, and school. And friends—friends from many nations of differing religions and cultures.

I think I only realized my life was different when returning to Denmark for holidays and visiting family, friends, and supporters. But I am not sure my life would have been better—or easier—growing up in Denmark.

Gitte Falk Jakobsen, Hannah & Egon's youngest child

My childhood was rich, exciting, unusual, carefree, and serious—all at the same time. While my parents always protected me from the scariest bits of life, I also always knew that whatever came our way, God would be a part of it—either as a blessing or as protection, shield, and help. The standard response to anything was always to turn to God—a habit if we can call it that, that I have taken with me into my adult life. Matthew 10:29 teaches us that "not a single sparrow can fall to the ground without your Father knowing it." (NIV). This has become a stable truth in my life and one that gives me comfort at all times. If God is concerned enough about small birds, how much more wouldn't He be concerned about me?

I have to admit, there have been times, though, where I wondered, did God really care? About me? Or was He only interested in the services of my parents? I knew without a shadow of a doubt that my parents had witnessed many miracles. I believed that they experienced the presence of God on a scale most other people might have found extremely intense. But I began to wonder, as a teenager, if I was just as interesting to God as they were. In time, I realized that I had to make an active decision to make the God of my parents become the God of me. I had to make it personal. As a young adult, I really struggled with that.

On the one hand, there was nothing I wanted more than to give God my life and serve him. On the other hand, I longed for what I believed was a normal life—to blend in, not be different, to just be at home in one place. But at one point, God told me that His grace was enough for me—that all I needed was Him.

2. Corinthians 12.9 -" My grace is sufficient for you, for my power is made perfect in weakness." (NIV). It was like he challenged me to come to rest, not because of a geographical place, a job, or a title, but to come to rest in Him—to accept that all I had ever really needed was Him. I believe this is what my parents have done. They have found their home in Him, and as a result, they have been able to follow the lead of the Holy Spirit in their lives.

When my husband and I married, we agreed that God would be the center of our marriage. Young and inexperienced at life, we desperately wanted God to be a tangible force in our lives. We were so blessed to become part of a church that shared our hunger for God. We experienced firsthand how God suddenly moved in miracles and healings in a small church in Denmark. We saw him change people's lives and give them joy where there was sorrow and peace where there was anxiety. I don't think there were any miracles as crazy and wild as some of the miracles in Tanzania, but is that really the point? For us, witnessing these miracles in our little church set us on our path as servants of God. We suddenly experienced the Holy Spirit in a way that must have equaled the intense presence my parents live with. And we were ruined for good—the taste of what God can do has eliminated all other desires. We have, up until now, spent our married life following His lead. We have been blessed and taken care of all these years. We have never lacked anything, although we are just ordinary, working-class people. We have served him and seen people be changed in his presence through worship, prayer, and just sitting in His presence. And we are still ruined for Him. Nothing and no one else will do for us.

God truly did take care of me—of us. He proved to me that His grace really is sufficient for me. No matter my history—good or bad—He has all I need. I believe the same is true for you.

Chapter Twenty-Three

MARRIED TO EGON

By Hannah Esbensen Falk

A long time ago—more precisely, 1st August 1965, we were young and only big kids; you were 17, and I was 15. We met in a youth camp on your island Bornholm.

I attended the youth camp the whole week; you were only there for the weekend because you had a job during the week. Besides, you didn't like going to church; it was boring to you. Your mom, however, came every night, and when she cooked breakfast for you in the morning, she worked on you to get you going. She talked about the songs and the preacher and told you how good the services were, but no!

Hannah Esbensen Falk, Egon's wife.

One morning, she told you that many beautiful girls attended the youth camp, especially two beautiful twin girls. That evening, you decided to go have a look at the girls, and I was the lucky twin who first caught your eyes and later your heart.

We were so young and crazy in love. When the camp was

over, I had to return to my home at the other end of Denmark. But we wrote letters. We kept the mailman busy—every day, a letter went either one direction or the other, and as soon one of us had a vacation, we went to visit the other.

I watched on TV the Danish Crown Princess give a speech toward her husband, the Crown Prince, on his 50th birthday, and I liked something she said to him and I "borrowed" it.

She said: *"I am happy you swept my feet away beneath me, not only for a short term but for life."*

Today you are 72—you still look good in jeans. You have a drawer full of colored socks—you are colorful in many different ways. You take good care of yourself; you don't drop your dirty clothes on the floor or go to bed without placing your trousers and shirt on a hanger. Your desk is orderly before your leave it, and you keep your life in order—I love that about you.

After we met, you made sure I moved to your island, Bornholm. I was only a young student attending school, and I had to graduate before I could move. First, my parents said no way, but when we stayed in contact and in love for more than a year and my parents understood you also loved Jesus and came from a good Christian family, they finally gave their permission. In order for me to move to Bornholm, I needed a job to support myself. You went to your family doctor, sat and waited your turn in his clinic, and

asked him if he needed somebody to help him in the clinic. He said no, but my wife needs help in the house, so you fixed a job for me, and I moved.

Later on, I was educated as a nurse assistant at the hospital, and during that time, you moved to another part of Denmark to serve your duty to the Danish military. No problem, you traveled all the hospitals in that part of our nation and found me a job and had me move again. Shortly after that, we got married and lived in two small rooms upstairs, 2nd floor, in a backyard with the bathroom downstairs and outside. Later on, it became

Norway, where you traveled as an evangelist, and finally Tanzania. You have taken me all over, through big cities and to small remote villages, to preach Jesus.

Where would I have been if I hadn't met you? You are an explorer, and you love adventures.

You have taken me everywhere: Asia, Norway, USA, Africa, and mostly Tanzania.

We have had hundreds of Gospel campaigns and preached to millions of people. We have built our ministry together: the Gospel part of which is New Life Outreach; the Bible School, Academy of Leadership; our church, New Life City Church; and the more social part is New Life Schools with students from baby class through primary school and secondary school. We also gave out food, helped drill for fresh water in our local neighborhood, and gave away tons of secondhand clothes.

We have managed a lot through 51 years, and you have been primus motor in it all.

Yes, you have had help from others, but you have been the

head. You are a well-known face in Tanzania. The police stop you on the road just to say hello, and people tell us they have watched you on the news because journalists attend our crusades where we give away different kinds of donations to local schools, hospitals, or other projects. I know this praise is not for you alone, but most of all toward our God.

| Hannah and Egon at a meeting campaign in Jordan.

We are blessed with three children, some wonderful daughter-and sons-in-law, and ten precious grandchildren.

Privately, you have a very soft heart. Your love for your children and grandchildren is enormous; you have a very soft heart. You always spend time playing with the grandchildren, and when we visit them, they run toward you and greet you first and me second. No bad feelings, I am happy to see this.

It takes a long time to get to know a person well, more than a lifetime. I know most things about you, but maybe not everything yet. But as long God knows your heart, it's enough for me. I am proud of you, proud of what you/we have accomplished. It takes a lifetime—with God's help.

You live for what you believe, and you are willing to die for what you believe. I know you want to die while preaching on your platform—many years from now.

You speak four languages besides the dialect that was spoken in Bornholm before 1969. After 1969, the dialect changed a lot and became thinner.

You were very shy as a child, and you still are in certain circumstances, even though it's hard to believe.

Thank you for sharing your life with me. I have no desire for anything else.

Love you dearly.

HELP MAKE A DIFFERENCE

Every single day New Life Outreach (NLO) makes a difference in Tanzania – one of the worlds poorest countries.

For more than 40 years, the NLO has been instrumental in shaping civil society, both socially and spiritually.

- NLO educates church planters at the Bible school.
- NLO holds evangelical campaigns in village areas.
- NLO has a girls' home for 25 vulnerable and orphans girls.
- NLO runs school for approx. 900 children. At the age of 3-17 years.
- NLO provides education to more than 300 children via sponsorships.
- NLO tells children & young people about Christianity.

You can give your financial support for the work of Hannah and Egon Falk by clicking on this donate button:

HELP MAKE A DIFFERENCE

Or scan this QR-code:

Support Hannah & Egon Falk QR-code

If you prefer using a check, then your financial support for the work of Hannah and Egon Falk can be sent to:

LIFE UNITED
P.O. Box 18862
Shreveport LA. 71138
Phone: 318 688 4411

Please make checks out to Life United, include a note saying it goes towards Egon Falk's ministry.

HELP MAKE A DIFFERENCE

Find out more about Hannah and Egon's work on:
WWW.EGONFALKMINISTRIES.COM

ABOUT THE AUTHOR

Evangelist Dr. Egon Falk is known for his Great Gospel Crusades throughout Africa and his help to the local tribes. He is also known as Africa's Billy Graham and is the author of several books, including *The Conquerors*.

Egon was born and raised in a fisherman's family on Bornholm, a small island in Denmark located in the Baltic Sea.

As a young teenager, he formed a Christian band, and they ministered all over the island during his education to become an engineer.

In the year of 1969, Dr. Egon Falk went into full-time ministry as a traveling evangelist.

He expanded his ministry in 1970 and moved to Norway.

In 1974, Dr. Egon Falk and his wife Hannah responded to God's call upon their lives to move to Tanzania, East Africa, and began their mission work.

They arrived with two small kids and a few belongings, and one year later, their third child was born in a small African village.

From a small and humble beginning, the ministry, New Life

Outreach, founded by Dr. Egon and his wife with more than 100 local co-workers, is now a well-known ministry all over Tanzania and even outside its borders.

The name of Dr. Egon has become a household name, and even though his name is not African, many African children are named Egon.

Dr. Egon and Hannah Falk have dedicated their lives to this great nation of Africa – especially TANZANIA.

Connect with Egon online:

- Author webpage: http://www.egonfalkministries.com
- Facebook: https://www.facebook.com/egon.falk
- Instagram: https://www.instagram.com/egonfalk/
- Linkedin: https://www.linkedin.com/in/egon-falk-54760a11b/
- YouTube: https://youtu.be/b-r58R-6XHw

www.ingramcontent.com/pod-product-compliance
Lightning Source LLC
Chambersburg PA
CBHW071432070526
44578CB00001B/84